Win from within!

Ted

Additional Praise for
So You Want to Start a Hedge Fund

There are virtually no books on the topic of how to pick individual hedge fund managers, so this is a must read for any asset allocator, whether a professional or a high net worth investor. In fact, all aspiring or current managers would also benefit from reading this book. Ted shares his wisdom from two decades of investing in hedge funds of all types and sizes, with particular insight into investing in early stage managers.

—Jonathan A.G. Auerbach, Hound Partners

There is no one better-equipped than Ted Seides to author a book on starting a hedge fund. From his early training at the Yale Investment Office to his instrumental role at Protégé Partners backing some of the best and brightest investment managers, Ted has forgotten more than most of us will ever know about the challenges of launching a fund. His refreshingly honest insights will resonate with readers of all backgrounds.

—David Z. Solomon, Managing Director,
Goldman Sachs Investment Partners

Ted Seides' extensive experience in identifying and supporting emerging hedge fund teams provides him with a unique insight into the hedge fund industry and valuable lessons for investors in the asset class. His book provides an interesting view into the challenges and opportunities for astute investors.

—Paula Volent, Senior Vice President for Investments, Bowdoin College

SO YOU WANT TO START A HEDGE FUND

SO YOU
WANT TO START
A
HEDGE FUND

Lessons for Managers and Allocators

Ted Seides

WILEY

Published by John Wiley & Sons, Inc., Hoboken, New Jersey.
Published simultaneously in Canada.

For general information on our other products and services or for technical support, please
contact our Customer Care Department within the United States at (800) 762-2974,
outside the United States at (317) 572-3993 or fax (317) 572-4002.

Wiley publishes in a variety of print and electronic formats and by print-on-demand.
Some material included with standard print versions of this book may not be included in
e-books or in print-on-demand. If this book refers to media such as a CD or DVD that
is not included in the version you purchased, you may download this material at http://
booksupport.wiley.com. For more information about Wiley products, visit www.wiley.com.

Library of Congress Cataloging-in-Publication Data:

ISBN 978-1-119-13418-3 (Hardcover)
ISBN 978-1-119-15697-0 (ePDF)
ISBN 978-1-119-15698-7 (ePub)

Printed in the United States of America

10 9 8 7 6 5 4 3 2 1

For Eric, Ryan, and Skylar (in alphabetical order),
My three most treasured start-ups.

CONTENTS

Foreword   xi
Acknowledgments   xv
Introduction   xix

  1 The Lessons   1
     Lessons for Managers   2
     Lessons for Allocators   4

  2 So You Want to Start a Hedge Fund?   7

  3 Attracting Capital   11
     Signals of Success   12
     A Classic Chicken-and-Egg Problem   30
     Investment Funds are Sold, Not Bought
     (Just Don't Tell the Buyers)   43
     Leveraging the Buzz   49

Contents

Riding the Wave   55

Building a Great Business   60

4   Team   65

Your Single Best Investment   66

The Best a Man Can Get   73

The Two-Headed Portfolio
Manager Monster   76

Where Do Nice Guys Finish?   83

Turnover: Don't Knock It Till You Try It   86

Pacing Growth   91

5   Investment Strategy   97

Finding True North   97

Best Foot Forward, With Both Feet   100

The Tug of War between Flexibility
and Style Drift   106

Stick to Your Knitting   117

Building Blocks of Process   123

6   Investment Performance   129

A Slave to Monthly Numbers   130

Sustaining Performance   134

Reaching for Return   138

The Role of Luck   144

The Best Month in a Manager's Career   150

Contents

7 So You Want to Invest in a Start-Up Hedge Fund?   153

Influencing Outcomes   154

Terms   158

Preparing for Bumps in the Road   164

Heed the Stop Sign   167

Crossing the Velvet Rope   173

Making Decisions   177

8 Parting Thoughts   183

Author's Disclaimer   189

About the Author   193

Notes   197

Index   205

FOREWORD

When I followed one of my mentors, Barton Biggs, in setting up my own investment firm a few years back I felt uniquely prepared to embark on that effort. After all, I had spent nearly a decade at one of the best run hedge funds in the business, a number of years at Morgan Stanley, one of the most important brokers servicing the industry, several years as a securities analyst covering the investment management industry and ten years teaching Ben Graham's Securities Analysis Class at Columbia Business School. Just through osmosis I got to know a number of folks who have built wildly successful investment operations. I even sat (and still sit) on the board of Rich Pzena's eponymous investment firm. What the heck else was there for me to possibly consider? Hang out my shingle, raise a few shekels and get on with it.

Well, before I rang that opening bell a friend of mine counseled that I should reach out and spend time with Ted Seides. I am glad I did. No one knows more about the start-up process for a hedge fund than Ted. He has become a key player in driving the growth of the modern hedge fund industry from its early stage as the popular new kid on the block, through awkward adolescence to the mature, institutional paradigm that dominates the landscape today. Ultimately, Ted not only became an important early investor in my fund but also a friend; I am immensely grateful to know him in both capacities.

Which brings me to *So You Want to Start a Hedge Fund*. Prior to college, I must have read every book ever published on baseball. Good (*My Turn at Bat*) or bad (*Super Joe—The Life and Legend of Joe Charboneau*) the combination of statistics and larger than life personalities sucked me in where fiction could not. When it became clear the Red Sox were not going to be in the market for a left-handed shortstop, I turned my literary focus to books on the investment world. I am not ashamed to admit it—I have read pretty much every book published on investing. From *People* magazine-like treatments of investment "stars" to the only true investment Bible— Ben Graham's *Securities Analysis* I must have read them all. Amazingly though, despite explosive growth in the hedge fund industry (there are now more hedge funds than stocks listed on the NYSE) and breathless coverage from the media that vacillates between fawning and *schadenfreude*, there have been virtually no insightful treatises on the inner workings of hedge funds. Until today.

So You Want to Start a Hedge Fund is the first book written by an insider that looks under the hood of the industry and offers thoughtful views on key success drivers and pitfalls—for asset allocators and managers alike. Effectively, through a combination of anecdotes, data and reasoned judgment, Ted has produced the first owner's manual for the hedge fund industry. Crucially though, this is not a cookbook. That is, there is no secret recipe inside that says start with a bag of dough, add some quantitative meat, season with experience and you have an alpha pie. As with picking stocks—while there may be basic True North principles in building (or selecting) an investment management business—there is also an immense amount of nuance to the process. Ted captures that here.

Ted has also seen firsthand virtually every mistake an investment entrepreneur can make. I now know—I made a bunch of 'em—most outlined vividly in this book. For the budding hedge fund manager—trust me—you will find your own creative and original mistakes to make, so you may as well use this book to avoid the more familiar ones. Indeed, one of my chief regrets is that Ted did not write the book three years ago so I could have read the galleys *before* I launched my firm. Not only might the knowledge imparted from *So You Want to Start a Hedge Fund* saved me time and effort—it would have kept me out of the damn book altogether as one of the proverbial cautionary tales.

Finally, while Ted accuses me of being one of the more likeable guys on Wall Street (which, to be clear, would merit a slander lawsuit from any number of today's hedge fund *Masters of the Universe*) it is obvious that *he* has to take the nice guy blue ribbon. After all, only Ted Seides could engender enough goodwill to get me to write a foreword to his first book after subjecting my firm to the financial equivalent of a colonoscopy in his due diligence process. What a wonderful business. It is captured superbly in the pages that follow—enjoy.

Steve Galbraith
Founder
Herring Creek Capital
Stamford, CT
October 12, 2015

ACKNOWLEDGMENTS

I want to take this opportunity to thank the people who influenced my career and led me down the path leading to this publication.

Many friends have been influential in helping me learn about myself, an essential characteristic for success in investing and in life. My parents, Jane and Warren Seides, have provided unconditional love and support through every mountain and valley on my journey. I am deeply indebted to Shari Greenleaf, Michael Mervosh, and Kali Rosenblum, each of whom has shared countless pearls of wisdom walking alongside me.

My investment education started under the tutelage of David Swensen and Dean Takahashi at Yale back in 1992. The building blocks of my knowledge came from their brilliant minds, scholarly approach, and teaching orientation. I was lucky to land in their offices upon graduating college and am grateful to have started my career working for a dynamic duo who imparted values of integrity, balance, and service that resonated strongly within me.

While at Yale, I met Charley Ellis, then a member of Yale's Investment Committee. Charley was one of the first investment luminaries who saw something in me I had not yet seen in myself. He encouraged me along the way, wrote a recommendation that helped me gain entry to business school, and overwhelmingly expressed his enthusiasm at this effort, just as he did when David wrote his seminal work 15 years ago. Charley is a masterful storyteller and a gracious man who knows how to make each person he is with feel like they are the most important one in the room; an admirable exemplar of presence to behold.

The team at Protégé Partners since its onset experienced these stories alongside me and contributed to my understanding of the lessons learned. I am indebted to my former colleagues for their hard work and challenging insights along the way.

Much of what I learned at Protégé came from our partnerships with money managers. Some are mentioned in this book and many others are not. You all know who you are, and you have my deepest gratitude for being the driving force behind Protégé's success.

INTRODUCTION

A little over two decades ago I had the good fortune to enter the working world under the tutelage of one of the world's greatest investors, Yale University's renowned chief investment officer David Swensen. David is a gifted teacher and provided an unparalleled investment education to everyone who had the privilege to work for him. His innovative investment ideas and disciplined framework established a foundation that my former colleagues and I built off in our own ways ever since.

From those early years in my career, I developed a passion for investing in people. One of Yale's many levers of success has been its extraordinary ability to partner with top managers across all asset classes in the start-up phase of their businesses. Helping someone at a key moment in their career and serving as a catalyst to realize their dreams resonated so strongly with me that it carried through my post-MBA path to the formation of Protégé Partners.

I have met so many passionate, intelligent, and high-quality people through my work the last 20 years that these pages could not give the vast majority justice. Some of these folks have become world famous—from my first manager meetings in 1992 with Jeremy Grantham and Tom Steyer to what became an infamous charitable wager with Warren Buffett. Many others have demonstrated fantastic investment success while maintaining a low profile in the investment world and next to none outside of it. Many more never achieved their lofty aspirations despite herculean efforts.

My role in this ecosystem afforded me the privilege of working with those I believed would be the best of the best and fostering those relationships over time. It should come as no surprise that many also have become friends. As I once told Warren, I invest in people—the smartest, hardest-working, and best ones I know. He responded, "I do the same thing."

THE SECRET SAUCE

I wish after all this time that I had a secret recipe to deliver success to deserving start-up investment funds. Unfortunately, no such recipe exists. A new fund in today's market faces an intensely competitive landscape in an industry with a preexisting cornucopia of products. Differentiating based on product or price has been tried in just about every way, shape, and form already.

A number of managers nevertheless launch successfully every year, thereby defying the odds for start-ups in aggregate. These firms create meaningful businesses that reward their clients, employees, and ultimate beneficiaries over time. The checklist of essential ingredients for the winners in this game appears generic on the surface— a record of success throughout life, ability to raise money, skill to generate excess returns, development of repeatable processes, creation of suitable infrastructures, attraction and retention of talented investment staffs, temperament and grit to weather challenging times, and good luck. This same set of characteristics describes more failures than successes, so the subtleties in executing each facet of the business matter.

This book seeks to describe some key lessons about the opportunities and risks facing start-ups using historical examples. These stories are not those you read about in the papers. Billionaire hedge fund managers who have reached the economic pinnacle of a lucrative field for the most part don't grace the pages of this book. Instead, the principals whose firms I discuss are all highly educated, well trained, talented, and competitive people who gave it their very best and either achieved success or fell short in its pursuit. I have focused on a slice of a fund's life when success was far from a forgone conclusion.

While I believe this work may prove useful to many, we all need to walk our own paths in investing and in life. As much as I have learned to rebuff the words *should* and *ought to* in following my path, these same words creep into this book frequently. Please take these words with a grain of salt—they are as much a reminder to me in my daily practice of investing as they are intended to be helpful tips for you.

Importantly, throughout the book, I have used male gender pronouns. The hedge fund industry is populated by more men than women, but the convention is intended solely for simplicity. Many high quality female managers and allocators pervade the industry as well as men.

WHY NOW?

The hedge fund industry is at a significant crossroads for both managers and allocators. The industry is maturing, aggregate growth is slowing, and competition is shifting from industry-wide growth at the expense of traditional asset classes to market share capture across hedge funds. The structure of the hedge fund industry is highly concentrated in the largest funds, and the big have been getting bigger. According to Hedge Fund Intelligence, only 305 hedge funds out of the 7,500 comprising the universe manage more than $1 billion.[1]

This increasing concentration is a consequence of the late-stage development of the industry. The money at the margin entering hedge funds tends to come from large pension funds. These pensions need to invest substantial dollars and face limitations on comprising too much of a single manager's business, leading them to focus only on large funds.

However, many of these large funds are overseen by a founder who generated substantial wealth for himself and is approaching retirement age. Firms with leaders older than 60 manage one-third of the assets in the industry and those with principals in their 50s comprise another third.[2] In time, some of these big funds will not survive their founders, and large sums will get reallocated to different managers. Most hedge fund organizations see this industry landscape evolving and try to position themselves for future growth. The lessons in this book may help small existing funds push the proverbial boulder up a challenging hill.

Each year, more managers try to enter the fray as well. A new coterie of talent, typically in the age range of 32 to 38, find themselves with the requisite knowledge, experience, capital, and hunger to strike out on their own. These budding entrepreneurs may have a mentor and some peers with whom they consult, but rarely have access to a wide assortment of prior mistakes made and lessons learned. I hope that sharing these stories will help new funds avoid the errors of some of their predecessors.

For allocators, "retirement risk" has created a need to rethink the composition of increasingly stale hedge fund portfolios. Existing investors in hedge funds across endowments and foundations, pension funds, sovereign wealth funds, financial institutions, family offices, and high-net-worth individuals will have quite different allocations to managers 5 or 10 years from now than the ones they have today. Allocators will need to assess funds in an earlier stage of development than they have historically to build a next generation portfolio. In its most recent annual Investor Survey, J. P. Morgan's Capital Introduction group noted this shift in attention.

> *In their search for alpha, institutional investors have moved down the assets under management ("AUM") spectrum, with three-quarters of respondents willing to invest in a hedge fund with $100 million or less. Along those same lines, approximately 70% of respondents are willing to look at a hedge fund manager with a track record of one year or less.[3]*

A dynamic, evolving hedge fund organization faces different challenges from a mature, large firm. Allocators are accustomed to recognizing the issues in large firms, but are less knowledgeable about those in smaller ones. In time, allocator behavior will shift away from the buy-and-hold investment decisions that have served them well with large funds. The stories in this book may help allocators avoid some of the mistakes I have made along the way.

My work in the past 14 years has focused exclusively on hedge funds, but this book takes no position on the popular debate about the merits of hedge funds for institutional and personal portfolios. While I am positively disposed, both bullish and bearish camps have compelling arguments. On the positive side, the hedge fund industry has undoubtedly attracted some very bright and talented people, and the majority of successful new investment organizations created over the past decade have been hedge funds. These firms have spent more resources on research and development (R&D) than any asset management businesses have in the past. Alpha may flow to where the talented young people reside and where resources are most aggressively deployed to mine for gold.

On the other hand, Charley Ellis astutely points out that the very intelligence and competitiveness of this class of people makes their success inordinately difficult to achieve as a group.[4] Competition has reduced many of the inefficiencies that hedge funds capitalized on in the 1980s and 1990s, and R&D spending may not result in the generation of expected returns.

I will set aside the debate with words of the late Peter Bernstein, who was fond of reminding us that "we don't know what will happen."[5]

VIGNETTES

I use stories of hedge funds I have partnered with or known about in my time in the business as fodder for this book. Rather than dive deeply into the history and strategy of the interesting leaders of each fund, a style employed by John Train in *The Money Masters*[6] and many who followed in his footsteps, I have chosen a vignette in the life of these funds to demonstrate a particular lesson.

By isolating one issue at a time, I have knowingly simplified the many factors that contributed to the success or failure of the fund. For example, the early chapters that focus on organization and momentum in raising capital leave out the necessary conditions for success of strong performance and an impressive team. Despite these limitations, taken together the anecdotes build a framework that many managers and allocators may find useful.

I hope these stories help lead you down a path of success, whatever that may mean to you.

1

THE LESSONS

LESSONS FOR MANAGERS

Attracting Capital

1. Be thoughtful before you speak to prospects.
2. Reflect often on how you present yourself.
3. Offer incentives to get all-important early wins.
4. Dedicate resources to facilitate the marketing process.
5. Create a brand and leverage the buzz.
6. Be prepared in advance and strike while the iron is hot.
7. Diversify your client base to build a great business.

Team

8. Investing in people is the best decision you can make.
9. Your organization will evolve, but your culture remains.
10. The two-headed portfolio manager is nearly extinct, so choose a structure more fit to survive.
11. Put your destiny in your own hands.
12. Make the changes you need to thrive irrespective of external perception.
13. Stay connected to the drivers of your success.

Investment Strategy

14. Be true to yourself.

15. When getting started, don't let perfect be the enemy of good.

16. Communicate frequently with clients to sustain a flexible strategy.

17. Anticipate the inevitable ebb and flow of a focused strategy.

18. Pay attention to process and outcomes will follow.

Investment Performance

19. Focusing on the short term is antithetical to achieving long-term success.

20. When you think you have arrived, your next adventure will have just begun.

21. If you fly too close to the sun, you're apt to get burned.

22. Never underestimate the role of luck.

Allocator Relationships

23. Mirror your potential partner to learn who he is.

24. Strive to give more for less.

25. Be frank about the challenges you face—teaching something of value may pay dividends down the road.

(Continued)

26. Share your honest assessment of the opportunity set in good times and bad.
27. When you strip away the label, an allocator's job is a lot like yours.

LESSONS FOR ALLOCATORS

Attracting Capital

1. Your time is precious—manage it well.
2. The early bird catches the worm.
3. Putting yourself in a manager's shoes may shed light where others see darkness.
4. Timing matters, so separate your decision to invest with a manager from your timing of when to invest.
5. Hot managers may cause you to gloss over important issues; cold ones may offer opportunities glossed over by others.
6. Follow your own voice when exiting managers.

Team

7. Prioritize talent development in your manager assessment.
8. Expect some ugliness inside the sausage factory.
9. Avoid marriages of convenience with a co–portfolio manager structure.

10. Don't be alarmed by change in a nascent organization.
11. Scrutinize your assumptions regularly when a firm grows quickly.

Investment Strategy

12. Write down your goals in advance, and make honest assessments of performance against those goals.
13. Investigate the quality of a manager's early results—you may find that some babies are thrown out with the bathwater.
14. Communicate thoroughly and openly with managers to develop a shared understanding of expectations.
15. Pay attention to process, and outcomes will follow.

Investment Performance

16. Your interactions may affect your manager's behavior.
17. You will chase performance, so make sure it is for the right reasons.
18. Focus on what matters most.
19. Recognize the difference between skill and luck.

Allocator Relationships

20. Be your best self in your relationships with managers.

21. Look to start-ups to extract better terms without adverse selection.

22. Adjust your mental model for the particular circumstances at hand.

23. When you fall in love, take your time.

24. When managers call for the ball, listen; when they run for the hills, proceed with caution.

25. Learn from the best by applying your managers' best practices to your investment process.

2

SO YOU WANT TO START A HEDGE FUND?

"Chase your passions, not your pension."

—Denis Waitley, author and motivational speaker

Seemingly every workday for the past 14 years, I received word that a friend; friend of a friend; or former peer, neighbor, or neighbor's peer's friend wants to start their own hedge fund. In each meeting, one of the first questions I pose is the same that all allocators will ask— why do you want to start your own fund?

The consistent answer among successful hedge funds takes on some version of "it's time." For some, this means they have developed the requisite skill set to manage money and have a burning desire to put their name on the door. Others yearn to break through the constraints placed on their investing activities, whether from liquidity, risk levels, or institutions. Still more are driven by the desire to compete at the highest levels and view starting a hedge fund as the apex of competition in the capital markets.

Successful hedge funds are driven by the passion of their founders. My high school wrestling coach used to bark "you've gotta want it" to my teammates and I in the heat of brutal workouts. Similarly, an aspiring hedge fund manager must be deeply committed to all aspects of both investing and building a business in order to succeed. Founders must tackle a multitude of tasks and headaches to run the business and simultaneously handle the intense pressure of managing money. Many do not fall into this camp and may want to reconsider how green the grass is underneath their feet.

The often unstated rationale for launching a hedge fund is the desire to make oodles of money. Money is an ephemeral motivator, and few driven solely by the pursuit of riches will compete successfully against those with an innate passion for the business independent of financial rewards.

Talented professionals approaching a launch for the right reasons with the requisite drive to build a business can take a series of steps to turn their ambition into reality. The nuts and bolts of the process are an accessible commodity, imminently learnable from perusing prime brokerage guides[1] or conducting a Google search on "starting a hedge fund." What follows is a set of more subtle lessons about attracting capital, organization, investment strategy, performance, and allocation from investing in and working with hundreds of hedge fund start-ups over the past fourteen years.

3

ATTRACTING
CAPITAL

From the moment a budding investment entrepreneur dreams of launching his own fund to the month he crosses a critical mass in assets, not a day will go by when capital raising is far from his mind. In a typical start-up, a manager is confident of his investment acumen and is blissfully unaware of the machinations of marketing. The process of raising capital is repeated by funds every year, but it is always new to the first-timer.

The fundraising process often begins when service providers to hedge funds point aspiring managers in the direction of potential capital providers. The path from that first step to the wiring of cash into the fund's account has no universal road map.

Traditional academic marketing's Four Ps (product, place, promotion, and price)[1] and Four Cs (customer, cost, convenience, and communication)[2] tend to be too generic to help in this process. Instead, implicit signaling, subtle selling, and effective branding are more important concepts to master.

SIGNALS OF SUCCESS

People with money to dole out are always very popular. Starting my career at the top of the food chain was something lost on me in my youth. I went to business school after five years working at the Yale Investments Office with the belief that the leading professionals in the money management industry were all inordinately nice people, as my professional experience to that point had left me without a single contrary example. When I moved from the middle of Connecticut to the middle of Manhattan, I soon realized that there was not enough time in the day to spend with all those friendly fund managers. My calendar often was fully booked two or three weeks at a time with manager meetings across our portfolio, leading prospects, and favors to clients and friends.

I was far from alone in this paradigm. Anyone with a checkbook has a steady stream of suitors, and gaining their attention is not easy to do. Allocators must take shortcuts to triage prospective investments in a universe full of talented professionals. The filtering process begins long before a manager walks in the door for a meeting. A manager's entire life path from education to fund launch gives signals that allocators infer to screen the plethora of inquiries they receive regularly.

While allocators protect their precious time, each manager sees himself as a worthy exception to the rule. Most emerging managers think their circumstances are differentiated and special. A start-up manager may tell a story about its unique strategy, past track record, and team cohesiveness, alongside a host of reasons why their start-up really isn't a typical one. An experienced allocator finds almost nothing that sounds unique, even though it may all seem so to the manager.

Managers are usually too optimistic about their prospects for attracting capital as a result of this disconnect. The industry is full of highly intelligent, highly talented, and highly motivated people, only a few of whom launch successful businesses. It is the very reality of how many amazingly talented people have found their way to the hedge fund industry that makes it so competitive.

In order to improve the odds of success, a manager should be thoughtful about the signals he sends to allocators in each stage of the process. Allocators pay close attention to a manager's preparation, introduction, meetings, and operations, and a manager can put his best foot forward by understanding the needs of allocators in advance. A manager can apply the same discipline and creativity to marketing that he does to investing.

Approaching Prospects

> "I've heard there are 8,000 hedge funds in the market. But I think there must be 32,000 because I've met 8,000 and they're all in the top quartile."
>
> —Mark Yusko, investment manager

Aspiring managers often worry about the importance of their historical track record, but allocators at this stage of the game pay far more attention to qualitative attributes. Very few successful start-ups come armed with audited track records, and only a few more have performance figures endorsed by their prior employer. Even then, allocators to early-stage funds take all prior records with a grain of salt. The set of precedent conditions under someone else's roof may not reflect those that a new manager will face when he goes off on his own.

Instead, allocators look to an individual's personal history to gauge their potential for future success. Allocators to early-stage funds will query a manager's family life, education, work experience, nonwork activities, financial wherewithal, and personal acquaintances in an effort to paint a mosaic of the opportunity. Performance statistics become a sideshow when a manager receives glowing endorsements for all the right reasons.

Personal relationships invariably create the best opportunity for a warm introduction; however, an individual's network may extend only to a narrow universe of prospects. The next best approach, like the initiation of my bet with Warren Buffett, engages the recipient with subject matter that may resonate.

The Inception of the Bet

Friends have often inquired about how my bet with Warren Buffett came to pass. On a slow summer day in 2007, I heard Warren had suggested that a group of hedge funds couldn't beat the market over time. I suspected the timing of his proclamation was poor, since the market traded near peak valuations in 2007, and hedge funds can have a salutary effect on institutional portfolios in bear markets. I decided to call him out with a challenge and see what would happen from there. In reaching out to him, I wanted to choose my words carefully, establish some credibility, and pique his interest. I decided to write an old-fashioned guy an old-fashioned letter.

> *Warren Buffett*
> *Berkshire Hathaway, Inc.*
> *1440 Kiewit Plaza*
> *Omaha, NE 68131*
> *Dear Warren,*
>
> *Last week, I heard about a challenge you issued at your recent Annual Meeting, and I am eager to take you up on the bet. I wholeheartedly agree with your contention that the aggregate returns to investors in hedge funds will get eaten alive by the high fees earned by managers. In fact, were Fred Schwed penning stories today, he likely would title his work "Where Are the Customers' G5s?"*

However, my wager is that you are both generally correct and specifically incorrect. In fact, I am sufficiently comfortable that unusually well managed hedge fund portfolios are superior to market indexes over time that I will spot you a lead by selecting 5 fund of funds rather than 10 hedge funds. You must really be licking your chops!

To be fair, my five picks are not the ordinary fund of funds you might read about in Barron's. Each has been trained in the discipline of value investing with a long time horizon and has experience vastly different from the crowd of fee gatherers in the industry. You might call them "The Superinvestors of Endowmentsville."

[redacted]

Without diving into detail, the managers of these funds selected or helped select hedge funds at [redacted]

I am flexible as to what stakes you propose. I would offer a typical "loser buys dinner at Gorat's," but I hear your going rates for a meal are higher than mine these days (though my wife and young kids might beg to differ).

Best of luck and I look forward to hearing your index selection.

Sincerely,

Ted Seides, CFA

I did not know Warren prior to this communication, but imagined proposing a bet in this way would intrigue him. The subject matter was one of keen interest to him, and the references to investment classics like *Where Are the Customer's Yachts?*[3] and his own "The Superinvestors of Graham-and-Doddsville"[4] would bear familiarity. The letter led to an entertaining correspondence that Carol Loomis described in a *Fortune* article entitled "Buffett's Big Bet."[5]

On the opposite end of the spectrum, the least effective form of marketing is generic spam, like the following unsolicited e-mails.

The Circular File

Allocators occasionally come across inbound solicitations that exemplify what not to say when reaching out to prospects. Almost immediately, these e-mails are tossed in the electronic version of a garbage can. Most solicitations in the Circular File make outlandish boasts that elicit comedic reactions.

The first two examples are actual e-mails whose authors might as well have claimed they invented the question mark. The e-mails, grammar, and typos are in their original form with only the sender's biographical information removed.

Example 1

> *November 2, 2010*
>
> *If seeding worth $50M can be secured before entering 2011, I believe that I can generate $200M as a return on capital by 2012.*
>
> *I am a contrarian value investor. But above all, I have accurately timed every major market movement over the past 3 years, including the market bottom. Outperforming nearly every single hedge fund manager over the past few years and effectively managing a completely (100%) leveraged portfolio, through an incredibly difficult trading environment, have uniquely*

prepared me to effectively manage a sizable fund, while maximizing return and minimizing risk.

Prior to the "market bottom", I established overweight positions in drastically undervalued financials. Below is a summary:

Historical Performance

12/2007 – Correctly anticipated upcoming economic downturn and prepared to raise capital (Bearish).

11/2008 – Finished raising capital at 0% via Credit Cards, etc. and began to indentify investment opportunities.

02/2009 – Fully invested. Went "all in" by taking an overweight position in what were at the time some of the most undervalued securities, in effect calling a bottom in the stock market (Bullish).

03/2009 – Market bottoms.

10/2009 – Reached peak portfolio valuation (well over 100% ROI).

12/2009 – Called a "range-bound, sideways market" for 2010 (Neutral).

01/2010 – Refinanced Credit Card debt at 0%.

05/2010 to 11/2010 – Market has been range-bound for the greater part of 2010, as suggested by my analysis from last year. Dow has been oscillating between 9500 - 11500.

In simplest terms, I got it right when it counted most.

I will be reaching out next week;

Unstated allocator response: Our parents taught us that when something is too good to be true, it usually is. Thank you for providing such a clear example.

Example 2

September 2, 2014

I am planning on starting a hedge fund which would invest in technology stocks.

I have a Ph.D. in Molecular and Computational Biology from the University of Illinois. This proves that I have a serious tech background.

> *With your help of providing seed funding for the hedge fund, I could start trading in technology stocks ASAP.*
>
> *PLEASE help me to launch.*
>
> *Technology runs in my blood. Technology is what I do.*
>
> *I guarantee returns of ~30% in the first year by investing in Apple, Facebook & Intel.*
>
> *I can make it happen. I promise.*
>
> *I can be reached at xxx-xxx-xxxx. I hope to hear from you. Thank you.*

Unstated allocator response: We've heard of the "KISS" principle, but this seems a little too easy. You may want to watch that language as well; with any success, the SEC will be reviewing your stated guarantees.

Example 3

In the third example, an e-mail carrying the unimpressive header "+132% strategic seed opp" enclosed a table that manifested flaws in its process and rendered the proposition a nonstarter. It doesn't take two decades of experience to recognize a repeated violation of self-imposed risk limits.

June 27, 2012

Table 3.1 Risk Management Slide

	Target	Current*	Thoughts
Gross exposure	Below 200%	215.9%	Keep long position at or below 100% equity
Net exposure	−10% −40%	3.0%	
Industry net exposure	Less than 10%	6 out of 9 industry groups within limit	High dispersion of returns within industry groups makes analysis key component to generating excess returns while still limiting industry risk exposure
Real time worst case portfolio scenarios limits	Less than 15%	14.5%	Based off real time worst case scenario analysis, assuming all portfolio positions had worst 1 day loss simultaneously
Company specific long position concentration limit	10%	10 largest long positions between 3.4%–10.2%	

(Continued)

23

	Target	Current*	Thoughts
Short position concentration limit	5%	Largest short is 5.8%	
Risk analyst overseeing real time, internal portfolio exposure and Concept One Portal	Former specialist & trader (NYSE) for 13 years; oversaw 15 traders; daily risk profile	In place	Analyst regularly communicates with both PMs on exposures. PMs have access to internal systems & prime broker portal in office & remotely
Manage volatility	Under 20% annually	28% annualized in 2011 (23% without August 2011)	Implementation of incremental processes since onset of European crisis should reduce volatility

Unstated allocator response: We understand that consistency is the hobgoblin of little minds, but you're only batting 38% on your own risk guidelines.

Lesson for Managers

Be Thoughtful before You Speak to Prospects

With so much noise hitting allocators every day, taking time to address each solicitation individually is a sensible tack. The best way to be well received is to be well introduced, so start close in with the people you know.

We learn best what to do by gaining an understanding of what not to do. Only a tiny percentage of the thousands of solicitations I reviewed over the years were as poor as those in the Circular File, but the worst of the worst makes clear that gaining a foot in the door of a crowded room takes more than a cold call or e-mail.

Signals in Marketing

> "It would be interesting to find out what goes on in that moment when someone looks at you and comes to all sorts of conclusions."
>
> —Malcolm Gladwell, author

Experts in body language teach that judgments about competence, trust, and integrity get formed almost instantaneously and are hard to change.[6] In addition to increasing the likelihood of getting in the door, a warm introduction puts an allocator in a better frame of mind to have a positive first impression.

A manager should market his fund employing the same principles he would espouse to an investor relations team at a public company. Transparency, analysis, and guidance can help allocators understand what they are buying. On the other hand, selective disclosure, unfocused messaging, and limited access can cause an allocator to pass just as quickly as an analyst would drop a stock idea for the next one. At every turn in the process, if an allocator can identify a reason to pass, he will move on to the next manager.

Once a manager gets inside, he encounters an allocator at the beginning of a complex decision-making process. At any moment in time, an allocator might range from being fully present and engaged to completely preoccupied and uninterested. The manager should approach stating their case in the same way a football quarterback plays offense. The goal of each meeting should be to move the ball down the field, with a first meeting leading to a second, a second to a third, a third to a fourth, and eventually to receive an investment at the goal line. Both a Hail Mary pass in a football game and trying to win a mandate in a single meeting hold low probabilities of success and take up precious time that might otherwise be spent moving closer to the end zone.

Almost every hedge fund of size is led by an articulate portfolio manager, and almost every start-up hedge fund that gets early traction has an engaging and insightful leader at the helm. Many other entrepreneurs may be just as good at managing money, but allocators typically associate clear, articulate presentation skills with clear, logical investment processes. The gift for gab can be a prerequisite for fund-raising success.

The opposite is also true. On many occasions, I sat with a prospective manager arising from a top-flight education, impeccable pedigree, and outstanding track record who nevertheless had the tendency to ramble on when presenting. Although many of these managers achieve a measure of success, more often than not their presentation style reflects their day-to-day time management and the working of their mind. Successful investing is competitive enough for those who don't get in their own way; the rest are unlikely to build a thriving business.

Signals in Operations

"High expectations are the key to everything."

—Sam Walton, businessman and entrepreneur

Operational excellence in hedge funds is a bit like going to the dentist. While absolutely necessary for a healthy business, the best an operations team can do is meet the expectations of demanding clients. The operations of a hedge fund command best practices, require evolving knowledge, and fall under intense regulatory scrutiny. Much like a tweaked gum line, one wrong step in operations can cause the loss of a prospect, the demise of a client, or even the end of a business.

Hedge fund managers should allocate sufficient resources to ensure operations run smoothly given the poor asymmetry in outcomes. The suite of best practices in operations can be readily identified through prime brokers, outsourced operational due diligence providers, peers, and prospects. In a mature industry, allocators will accept only the highest standards.

Lesson for Managers

Reflect Often on How You Present Yourself

In the midst of the busiest time in a young fund's life, a manager ought to take a step back and think carefully about the signals his actions give to prospective investors. Whether in preparation, setup, or meetings, every interaction will be scrutinized and compared to the best in the industry.

Lesson for Allocators

Your Time Is Precious—Manage It Well

Allocators are often well attuned to the signals sent by aspiring managers. Their need to sort the wheat from the chaff is part of their daily work, and most have developed implicit or explicit rules to increase the probability of success. When traversing a less familiar landscape like emerging managers, allocators should make these rules explicit, identifying in advance the type of leader, organization, and strategy with which it seeks to partner.

A CLASSIC CHICKEN-AND-EGG PROBLEM

"Which came first, the chicken or the egg?"

—Philosophical thought experiment

Getting a small hedge fund off the ground poses a classic chicken-and-egg problem. Most allocators will only spend time investigating a fund that has grown to critical mass; therefore, a fund that has not reached that level cannot get the attention of most allocators. Dedicating resources and sending the right signals can lay the foundation for a fruitful fund-raising effort, but only money in the bank pays the bills.

The legions of funds that do not launch with a big splash have three routes to influence the trajectory of their business:

- Bootstrap step by step
- Jump start with a seed investor
- Kick-start with discounted terms

Bootstrapping

Although most of today's multibillion-dollar hedge funds started as bootstrapped operations, the industry is more competitive and less forgiving than it once was. Every so often, a hedge fund emerges from the ashes to become a formidable business. When this happens, it is preceded by an unusually strong stretch of performance aligned with all of the raw material to create a brand. In that way, the bootstrapping strategy contains an implicit bet on performing substantially better than others in a crowded field—not an easy task, to say the least. A bootstrapped launch can place enormous stress on the business leader to make ends meet.

Flowering Tree Investment Management[7]

Rajesh Sachdeva, an affable Indian with an easy smile and booming professorial voice, left the hedge fund Sansar Capital in early 2008 to set out on his own. Rajesh had spent a decade focusing on Asian investments between the sell side and buy side before joining Sansar at its inception. Like the stocks he followed through repeated financial crises in the region, he fully expected that his path to growing a successful fund might be a rocky one.

While waiting out his contractual garden leave, Rajesh watched as Sansar suffered a significant drawdown in the fall of 2008. As a result, his once well-regarded past had dropped a notch in the esteem held by the allocator community. He launched in May 2009 with personal capital set aside and a team of 10 ready to go. Rajesh expected $30 to $40 million to show up, but when push came to shove, his Flowering Tree Investment Management launched with just $12 million from friends and family.

The first step in Flowering Tree's development was Rajesh's internal struggle to manage expectations. He was devastated by the absence of outside capital at launch. Rajesh felt he had set expectations reasonably, and even then he had been too optimistic. This cold splash of water was incredibly painful for him emotionally. Month after month, he felt the stress of writing a check out of his pocket to fund the business expenses.

Rajesh soon had to make an important decision that pitted the reality of the business against a suboptimal growth opportunity. A few months into Flowering Tree's life, a couple of prospects told Rajesh that they would be interested in taking their diligence to the final stage if he would consider offering monthly liquidity with no lockup on the capital. Rajesh sensed that these investors might be proverbial "hot money" and a poor fit for his strategy, so he turned away the offers. While he believed the decision would best position the firm for long-term success, his rebuffing of needed working capital put that much more pressure on him, and his team questioned whether he should have sacrificed his ideals for the survival of the business. As long as he decided to hold out, Rajesh faced a constant tension between doing the right thing for the portfolio and the right thing for the business.

Investment strategies commonly are starved for capital just when the opportunity set is best, and Flowering Tree's launch was proving to be another example of this phenomenon. When blocking out the stress of the business, Rajesh saw fantastic investments in his portfolio. Through his team's good work, investment performance was outstanding.

Flowering Tree got its first big break just shy of a year after launch. While unsuccessfully attempting to woo high-net-worth individuals and family offices that might invest a few million dollars, two institutional investors that had taken a passing interest started engaging in their diligence. One wrote a small check and began a regular dialogue that would later prove fruitful. A few months later, the other invested $40 million in exchange for a fee discount. The investment in February 2010 gave the organization hope and a faint light at the end of the tunnel.

It took another year before Flowering Tree hit its second important milestone. The first institution that invested in small size continued a dialogue with Rajesh every month. After nearly a year of conversation and a year and a half post-launch, they ramped up and became Flowering Tree's largest investor. The investment brought firm assets above the breakeven level of $130 million, allowing the organization to breathe a little easier.

Two Sansar clients invested in Flowering Tree in 2011, marking a third key milestone. These investors removed the last easy reason for prospective investors to say no. Soon thereafter, Flowering Tree started winning over investors at a steady, measured pace. By the end of 2011, assets had grown to $400 million.

As often occurs in a bootstrapped launch, Flowering Tree needed to perform well for a long time before allocators took notice. Rajesh watched investors withdraw from Sansar after 2008 and chose to be patient getting prospects comfortable with Flowering Tree. He felt pressure to accept capital that might be suboptimal for his portfolio management process. As he recalls, "The potential for it to mess with your mind and interfere with the portfolio management process is real. My biggest success was separating the two."

When Flowering Tree reached $500 million in assets under management (AUM) toward the end of 2012, it closed to new investors and began accepting only longer-duration capital that matched its investment horizon. The firm managed $600 million at the end of 2014 and had generated outstanding performance for its stable base of clients.

Seed Capital

Just as a company can sell equity as a path to finance growth, a hedge fund can attract a seed investment to provide working capital through the payment of management and incentive fees. Seeders work extensively with small funds and can provide strategic advice on team building, marketing, risk management, and operations. Additionally, seeders are members of the allocator community and can be instrumental in building momentum around a new fund launch.

That being stated, seed partnerships are not for everyone. A natural tension can arise between the manager's desire to focus on performance and a seeder's interest in asset growth to monetizing the value of the business. Alternatively, a manager may grow to resent paying a seeder should the fund prove successful. Managers may also find that some potential investors eschew funds that have seed partners.

No two seeders are alike, and a manager should attempt to align with a seeder that shares his vision for the fund and business. Managers and seeders together should construct the arrangement to enable continued connectivity in a mutually beneficial way as the years roll on.

One challenge in acquiring seed capital is that despite the seemingly large amount of it available, most of the money sits with only a handful of providers. The supply of potentially seeded funds far outstrips the demand for new managers from active participants in the space.

Pocock Capital[8]

In the spring of 2003, Joe Rantz considered launching his own fund. A Washington University graduate and crew rower who learned the trade of distressed debt investing at Farallon Capital, Joe later went on to manage portfolios at two smaller hedge funds. Joe developed an investment strategy to seize opportunities in a niche marketplace and delivered three years of commendable results. However, he had limited interaction with potential investors and did not know where to start.

Joe remained in close contact with his former colleagues and one of them introduced him to a seeder that had expressed an interest in his specialty. From that introduction came a lengthy diligence process and the beginning of a relationship that lasted over 10 years. Joe describes some of the benefits of working with a seeder:

> *I entered discussions with my seeder in the summer of 2003 with the desire to have a stable pool of capital to manage, but no appreciation for the scope of demands that starting an asset management firm would entail. As a trader and portfolio manager, it's easy to imagine the money just coming in from elsewhere and investing it. The marketing and operations side of the business is largely viewed as "someone else's problem." So for Pocock, the partnership made all the sense in the world. Leveraging off of their knowledge that had been built up and tested through several seed relationships, I could effectively leapfrog a lot of growing pains and implement best practices across several aspects of the business where otherwise I would have been flailing in the dark.*

I can see some managers feeling that the business assistance from a seed investor comes at too steep a price and resenting the fee sharing over time. But for me, the ongoing partnership with my seeder has proven invaluable as a source of advice and feedback both early on and over a decade since.

Joe's story is a common one for start-up managers. Many prefer to leverage a seeder's knowledge about building a hedge fund and are willing to trade off economics in exchange for maximizing the chance of success.

Discounted Terms/Founders' Shares

Shortly after the 2008 financial crisis, capital was particularly scarce for start-up hedge funds. At the same time, a wave of experienced traders from Wall Street proprietary trading desks sought to spin out and form new hedge funds. Bridging the gap between bootstrapping and seeding, "founder's shares" entered the industry lexicon. Founder's shares institutionalized the informal process of offering discounted fees to early adopters, as managers sought to raise a limited amount of capital in a finite time period after launch. These shares serve a similar purpose to seed capital in creating a critical mass with economic incentives for early adopters.

Founder's shares have both strengths and weaknesses for managers relative to seed capital. On the positive side, founder's shares are a less expensive means to the same end. The manager also has room for more than one investor to dip their toe in the water, providing a broader client base for potential follow-on capital once he proves his merit. However, founder's share investors are less committed to the new fund than a seeder, generally investing fewer dollars with a shorter lockup.

Redmile Group[9]

Five years ago, well before his firm had grown into a health care hedge fund with $1 billion in AUM and before the industry had created the concept of founder's shares, Jeremy Green faced a classic chicken-and-egg dilemma. An engaging Brit who started on Wall Street as a health care analyst, Jeremy launched Redmile Group in 2007 after successful stints over four years on the buy side focusing on health care stocks at Andor Capital and Steeple Capital. After raising $150 million out of the box, the fund generated strong performance in its initial two years, but nevertheless struggled to get investors to cross the finish line beyond the initial raise. Not only was Redmile a small, lightly staffed organization, but also its particular focus on health care narrowed the pool of potential investors relative to a generalist strategy.

Toward the end of 2009, Jeremy had three institutional investors conducting full-blown due diligence, but none of the three appeared ready to pull the trigger at the turn of the year. Rather than aggressively pursue the prospects or wait passively for lightning to strike, Jeremy got creative. One by one, he softly inquired where the investors stood and what might help them bring closure to their process. In one instance, he surmised that the institution would take more comfort in the company of additional institutional investors beyond Redmile's initial investors. In another, it appeared that cash availability was tight. With the last, he found a willing investor who preferred a separately managed account to an investment in Redmile's commingled fund.

In hopes of seizing the opportunity, Jeremy came up with a clever solution. He offered the likely allocator a managed account within a year, contingent on the fund growing to $250 million and the investor doubling their initial investment of $25 million. He also offered a fee reduction on the initial investment tranche. The investor took him up on the agreement and allowed Jeremy to offer comparable terms to the other two prospects so long as they invested a like amount on January 1, 2010.

Jeremy surmised that neither of the other prospects would be able to turn on a dime and invest, but he rightfully understood that both would greatly appreciate his overture. The events that followed met his best expectations. First, the prospect that preferred to be alongside another investor allocated a similar amount within three months. Soon thereafter, the cash-strapped prospect accessed funds and invested as well. By 2011, Redmile had more than doubled to $400 million and closed to new investors.

Jeremy's thoughtfulness in engaging his potential partners to meet their needs worked in spades. He explored a deeper understanding of his potential clients' process and astutely assessed their willingness and ability to allocate to Redmile.

Lesson for Managers

Offer Incentives to Get All-Important Early Wins

(Continued)

For most start-ups, creating incentives for early investors is a sensible path. Whether through a seeder or founder's shares, preferential terms can align the manager and early adopters to encourage growth. As the industry faces scrutiny on fees, the opportunity to offer something that clients are actively seeking is a win-win proposition.

If a manager canvasses a wide range of potential investors, he will encounter both supporters and critics of seeding and discounted shares. Among the pools of capital invested in hedge funds, the fund of funds community tends to embrace founder's shares more actively than others. In doing so, funds of funds have a place in the industry ecosystem by providing R&D for the industry. Except for the fortunate few whose brand allows a mega-launch, a start-up needs flag wavers in its corner to create positive signaling effects and branding. Both seeders and founder's share investors can help.

Lesson for Allocators

The Early Bird Catches the Worm

Allocators are best able to lower the fees they pay by investing in the early stages of a fund's life. The balance of supply and demand in small and emerging manager investing is tilted in favor of allocators. Those allocators willing to stand apart from the crowd will find a wealth of opportunity to negotiate better terms than those available with established funds. Should the allocator come upon a great fund, those terms can help generate higher net returns for many years.

INVESTMENT FUNDS ARE SOLD, NOT BOUGHT (JUST DON'T TELL THE BUYERS)

> "If a tree falls in the forest and no one is around to hear it, does it make a sound?"
>
> —Philosophical thought experiment

Start-up managers routinely underestimate the laborious process of raising capital. Unlike 20 years ago when it was reasonable to expect that a manager could perform well and eventually attract capital, today the law of large numbers in a crowded marketplace dictates that someone is always doing fantastically well. Performance is no longer enough; managers must also sell their story effectively to succeed.

Experienced and credible salespeople can make a big difference in the trajectory of a small fund. Good ones are relationship driven and have ongoing conversations with a large number of allocators to understand their needs. They are able to penetrate the allocator community and benefit from idea sharing among investors. Good marketers sell gently, recognizing that an allocator's job is manager selection, and most repel from a hard sell. Investment funds are indeed sold, but each buyer should be respected as an individual decision maker with a wide array of options.

Brenner West Capital[10]

A glimpse at Brenner West Capital might suggest that the firm has it all figured out. Ten years after its launch, principals Craig Nerenberg and Joshua Kaufman manage $1.5 billion in assets, are closed to additional capital, and have amassed a stellar track record. Brenner West also epitomizes just about everything that is right about the hedge fund industry. Unlike what you read in the daily papers, Craig and Josh are conservative, humble, and self-effacing.[11] Their firm name emanates not from grandiose mountains, voracious animals, or lofty aspirations, but rather from Craig and Josh's middle names.

Both Craig and Josh have spent their entire professional lives analyzing companies and demonstrate a deep passion for tearing apart businesses and complex investment situations on a daily basis. Craig started his career as a high school junior at Bill Ackman's first hedge fund, Gotham Partners. Josh entered the business at Goldman Sachs' investment banking program after college. Within a few years, the two connected under the same roof at Michael Dell's family office, MSD Capital, and in 2005 decided to launch their own fund. Brenner West's first decade proved a great success. The firm delivered market-beating returns and a true partnership with openness, transparency, and a shared vision of the investment program.

Despite the evident success today, it took six years for just about anyone to care.

With essentially the same personnel, investment process, and results that eventually attracted capital, Brenner West managed less than $150 million for its first five years and struggled to get anyone else interested in the fund. Their presentation was clear and understandable, their investment examples powerful, and they carried the added panache of managing capital for three generations of Ackman family members.[12] Yet no one took notice.

The lack of growth became a painful self-fulfilling prophecy. When Craig and Josh spent time investing, they saw tangible results, received positive reinforcement, and were empowered to do more. When they spent time marketing, they saw no results, felt negative reinforcement, and stopped spending time on the fruitless effort. By spending less time, the odds increasingly stacked against them.

Brenner West might still be a tree falling in the forest were it not for their timely hiring of marketer Alasdair Noble in 2010. A young man with something to prove, Alasdair spent all of his time seeking out prospects for the high-performing fund. Importantly, by the time he was ready to tell the Brenner West story, the fund had rebounded from a challenging 2008 with eye-popping returns in 2009 and 2010. It followed that year with a strong start in 2011, which laid the groundwork for investors to take notice of a terrific five-year track record. Alasdair started with his personal network, engaging two previous relationships to take a real look at Brenner West. Once those prospects peered under the covers, they liked what they saw, and capital started coming in the door. In short order, Alasdair reengaged other allocators that had casually window-shopped, and the process began to bear fruit.

Brenner West's great long-term record and short-term pizzazz pushed intrigued prospects across the finish line. Brenner West tripled its AUM to $450 million by the end of 2011 and closed its doors to new capital to digest the increase in assets. A year later, it reopened and saw excess demand, closing the fund at $1 billion. At the end of 2013, it raised a new tranche, experienced excess demand once more, and grew to $1.5 billion.

Lesson for Managers

Dedicate Resources to Facilitate the Marketing Process

Marketing and client service are time-intensive processes, and most funds do not grow without a dedication to the effort. In this day and age, hedge funds are sold, not bought.

Start-up funds often pile all the noninvestment activities on the shoulders of the same person. Portfolio managers eventually figure out that the personality genotype of most top notch accountants is quite a bit different from that of a successful marketers.

The importance of a thorough marketing and client service effort continues throughout an investment firm's life. Many of the largest and most successful hedge fund firms dedicate substantial resources to marketing and client service. Notably, Bridgewater Associates and AQR Capital have renowned client service efforts and have scaled their businesses enormously. No doubt this focus has been a causal variable in their successful growth.

Lesson for Allocators

Putting Yourself in a Manager's Shoes May Shed Light Where Others See Darkness

Many allocators do not appreciate how marketing and client service are an integral, ongoing, and essential allocation of time for 90% of managers, 90% of the time. Allocators want to believe that the best funds are focused solely on investing and choose to remain small. While many appear that way on the outside, it is rare for a manager to see merit in a stagnant organization.

Allocators wonder if an undiscovered manager is for real, commonly asking, "If the manager is so good, then why isn't it bigger?" The quandary is reasonable to ponder, but its answer may not be reflective of the fund's merits. Allocators to early-stage managers should challenge the assumption that size is a reflection of quality and consider that many funds choose not to spend resources on marketing, have not realized the importance of doing so, or have not articulately described the drivers of their success. Allocators should follow their instinct when researching smaller funds and worry less about the wisdom of crowds.

LEVERAGING THE BUZZ

"Success comes from taking the initiative and following up. … What simple action could you take today to produce a new momentum toward success in your life?"

—Tony Robbins, motivational speaker and life coach

I vividly recall a case study in my first year at Harvard Business School about the launch of the BMW Z3 Roadster in 1996. The marketing team at BMW used an array of innovative platforms to generate buzz about the sleek vehicle. Starting with a product placement in the James Bond film *GoldenEye*, the BMW team conducted a press launch in Central Park, a feature on the company's very first web site, a spot on Jay Leno's *Tonight Show*, and a campaign across the country to radio DJs to effect what the team referred to as "leveraging the buzz" created by the Bond film.[13]

Early-stage hedge funds that get noticed by the allocator community experience a common pattern. First, the fund attracts the attention of a small number of early adopters. Second, the manager leverages the buzz and soon finds packs of like-minded allocators eager to be "first to be the second investor." Third, investment returns follow that catch the eye of a growing number of prospective clients.

Successful leveraging of the buzz can follow recent academic research about the social process of spreading investment ideas. Most investors are passive receivers of ideas from a small number of leaders. When faced with a complex decision, allocators have the tendency to simplify the equation, at times substituting the merits of the investment opportunity for their trust in the introducer of the opportunity.[14]

This filtering process implies that a manager can create buzz through the company he keeps. John Maynard Keynes likened investing to a beauty contest, in which the judges focus on the likely opinions of the other judges rather than their own assessment of the participants.[15] A manager might choose to consort with his "hot" friends, those managers whose recent performance has put them in the good graces of their clients. A referral from a well-regarded manager can carry a lot of weight in building momentum. Just like back in high school, hanging out with popular friends can make a manager appear more attractive in the eyes of his desired audience.

Agecroft Partners

Managers who amass assets by leveraging the buzz create their own brand. Don Steinbrugge, founder of third-party marketing firm Agecroft Partners, believes that brands are the proximate driver of fund flows in the industry. Having spent the formative part of his hedge fund career running marketing at multibillion-dollar Andor Capital, Don created Agecroft to help a select group of undiscovered funds grow and has had great success in that endeavor. A number of his nascent funds later joined the billion-dollar club.

In a thoughtful expose entitled "Hedge Fund Branding Continues to Drive a Majority of Asset Flows," Don defines a hedge fund brand as "an investor's perception of the overall quality of a hedge fund." A small number of funds launch every year with great fanfare. These high-profile start-ups have already established a brand at their previous firm, are known to allocators in advance, attract a significant amount of publicity without effort, and launch with a large amount of committed capital.

For everyone else, Don believes there are three critical steps to create a brand and raise assets in today's competitive environment:

> *The first step in the process is having a high quality product offering … (including) a firm's operational infrastructure, investment team and their pedigree, investment process focused on their differential advantages, risk controls, performance, service providers and fund terms. A weakness in any of these factors can eliminate a firm from consideration. …*
>
> *The second step in the process of building a strong brand is making sure the market's perception of the firm is equal to (its) reality. This requires a consistently delivered, concise and linear marketing message that identifies the differential advantages across each of the evaluation factors investors use to select hedge funds. … The marketplace is highly competitive and hedge fund investors use a process of elimination in selecting hedge*

*funds. ... It only takes one poorly worded answer
to get a firm eliminated from consideration. ...*

*The final step in building a strong brand is
implementing a highly-focused marketing and sales
strategy that broadly penetrates the marketplace
while being compliant with regulatory guidelines.
The hedge fund investor marketplace is highly
inter-connected. Many investors exchange ideas on
managers and, as a result, the more deeply a manager penetrates the marketplace the stronger their
brand will become. Building a strong brand and
raising assets takes time and cannot be rushed. ...
In many instances, being too aggressive will elimi-
nate a firm from the selection process.[16]*

Managers often do not appreciate the subtleties that
differentiate those that create effective brands from
those that do not. Each step of the process must be done
with thought and precision in order to stand out from a
crowded pool of competitors.

Lesson for Managers

Create a Brand and Leverage the Buzz

Effective branding and leveraging the buzz can make the difference between a successful capital raise and an unsuccessful one. Part of the branding exercise postlaunch comes from the written communication that a manager shares with investors. The better the written word, the more allocators will gain interest on their own time.

Lesson for Allocators

Timing Matters, So Separate Your Decision to Invest with a Manager from Your Timing of When to Invest

Implicit in a manager's leveraging the buzz is the tendency of allocators to follow crowds, which often goes hand-in-hand with chasing performance. In every instance of assessing a small manager, an allocator should be keenly aware of what is drawing him to the manager at that particular moment in time.

Allocators should separate the decision about investing with a manager from the timing of doing so. Boards and clients put pressure on allocators to perform. The risk of investing with a talented fund after an unusually good period of performance is the possibility that a subpar period of performance will follow.

RIDING THE WAVE

> "A body in motion will stay in motion, unless acted on by an external force."

> —Sir Isaac Newton, physicist and mathematician

Once a manager raises an initial tranche of capital, he should continue to build on the momentum. The combination of early adoption and momentum enables an undiscovered manager to reach escape velocity as a business.

Momentum is a little appreciated and vitally important aspect of the fund-raising process. Allocators attend the same conferences, discuss hot new ideas with their peers, and gravitate toward strong recent performers. A manager can recognize this buying pattern and work to keep its name in the mix in the allocator community.

Breaking through a critical mass of assets in the early years can make or break the long-term success of a start-up. Funds that do not build on early momentum often struggle to reach the next level for years to come. As Don Steinbrugge describes:

Many small to mid-sized hedge funds become frustrated because their firm's assets under management are not growing ... Frequently they hear that once they get to a certain asset size, it will be much easier to raise assets. However, that is not necessarily true. ... Momentum in asset growth is more important to being successful in raising hedge fund assets for small and medium sized hedge funds than the current asset size of the organization. ...

If a firm is not growing despite a continued strong track record, investors will be reluctant to invest because they (presume) there must be a reason why other investors are not investing in the fund. As a result of this phenomenon, success in asset raising is much more likely for a fund that has grown from $100 million to $300 million over the past year than a $1 billion hedge fund that has had no asset growth (of late). In addition, raising assets for hedge funds is not a linear process, but is exponential.[17]

The power of momentum is as much of a driving force in hedge fund business building as it is in physics. Managers that seem to do everything right may still struggle to raise capital if not properly positioned to keep momentum in motion.

Seven Locks Capital[18]

Andrew Goldman's trajectory at Seven Locks Capital shows the importance of momentum in fund-raising. Andy trained as an investment banker and hedge fund analyst, and later served as a portfolio manager with multibillion-dollar AUM hedge fund Magnetar Capital. He struck out on his own in 2009 with two deputies who had worked alongside him previously. Seven Locks received a seed investment and got off to a sound start, generating steady returns from 2009 to 2011. The returns were good, but not good enough on their own to build momentum among the prospects he reached in the early going.

Starting in 2012, the portfolio began manifesting the results of Seven Locks' process and impressive returns followed. The firm delivered a strong return in 2012, followed by a monstrous 2013. In early 2014, the firm doubled its assets with a large investment from well-known family office, and got off to a very strong start to the year. In the spring of 2014, Seven Locks hired a dedicated marketer.

Much like Brenner West, Seven Locks had a few solid years of performance and then two and a half great ones. Both firms had impressive track records at the five-year mark, and told compelling stories of how their team and process combined to produce results.

But unlike Brenner West, Seven Locks' new marketer had very little time in the saddle to leverage the buzz before the fund experienced a soft patch of returns in the back half of 2014. Just as assets starting coming in the door, Seven Locks gave back half of its gains for the year over a few months. The performance itself, alongside little change in the portfolio and ostensibly none in the team or process, took away some marketing momentum just as Seven Locks' marketer ramped up outbound efforts. Over time, the event may prove little more than a speed bump, and the firm may now be better prepared should the next wave of strong performance elicit interest from allocators. Until then, the story provides an acute example of the importance of a manager having all of his ducks in a row.

Lesson for Managers

Be Prepared in Advance and Strike While the Iron Is Hot

Investment performance is not predictable over any short period of time, yet a start-up manager needs to capitalize on performance momentum to raise assets. The only way to strike while the iron is hot is to be fully prepared ahead of time.

Lesson for Allocators

Hot managers may cause you to gloss over important issues; cold ones may offer opportunities glossed over by others.

Similar to lessons learned from other examples in a manager's marketing process, allocators should be conscious of the timing of their investment decisions. A manager riding a wave of success may elect to close the fund to additional investors. An allocator who is excited about the long-term potential of the manager must choose between chasing performance, at least in the short-term, and eschewing the manager in pursuit of another without a recent performance windfall.

At the same time, very few allocators stand alone and invest in an undiscovered fund whose track record does not yet speak to its potential. Whether a start-up or a fund with stalled growth, capturing a fund ahead of a period of terrific returns is the road less traveled.

BUILDING A GREAT BUSINESS

"Be careful what you wish for, lest it come true."

—Proverb

Almost all start-up managers aspire to win over a group of clients who understand their approach, are long-term oriented, and own their capital. In an ideal world, these clients also are so busy that they generally leave the manager alone.

Almost every allocator presents himself to managers as a long-term investor with the wherewithal to withstand portfolio volatility en route to long-term success. History nevertheless demonstrates that few allocators act this way when the heat is on.

Diversified businesses generate higher-quality earnings streams than single-product business, and hedge funds are similarly stronger businesses with a diversified client base. Conventional wisdom holds that capital from an endowment or foundation is preferable to an investment from a fund of funds, or that a U.S. private client is better than a European one. These judgments may have been true on average historically, but we all know the story about the six-foot man who drowns in a river measuring four feet on average. Each investor in a start-up will be idiosyncratic and may not reflect the behavior of an average investor in their peer group. Start-ups by definition have more supply than demand and therefore often are not positioned to pick and choose their clients. The best a start-up manager can seek to accomplish is to find prospective clients who appear to have taken the time to appreciate its approach and who seem to have acted sensibly in other manager relationships. The manager will not know which clients stay true to their stated intention of maintaining a long relationship until a period of stress unfolds.

Endowment Capital Group[19]

In 2004, Philip Timon spun out of concentrated value fund Downtown Associates to launch his own business. Since his graduation from the University of Pennsylvania, Philip had developed a passion for analyzing businesses. He helped build a loyal following for Downtown that included some leading endowments. In particular, he found that the endowments had a deep understanding of his approach, a long time horizon, and control of their capital base. He believed this group of allocators constituted the ideal partners for his long-term, concentrated form of investing. As his initial marketing to these prospects gained traction, he named his firm Endowment Capital Group to further brand his intended prospect list.

Philip had the good fortune to leverage his outstanding track record to successfully raise capital from a group of nine endowments and foundations. He collected $200 million, with commitments to double that amount at launch and promptly closed the fund to new investors. By 2006, Endowment Capital Group grew through appreciation to nearly $500 million in AUM.

Following an off year in 2006 and another subpar year in 2007, one of the thought leaders among Philip's client base made the decision to exit the fund, citing a host of business and performance issues. What followed shortly thereafter was unthinkable to Philip upon Endowment Capital's launch; one by one the presumably independent-thinking, long-term-oriented endowments and foundations also exited the fund the same year. Philip did what clients asked of him, bringing in an experienced CEO to run the business and retaking exclusive control over the portfolio. Even then, all of the large clients but one exited at the proverbial bottom in 2008.

The lone stalwart left Endowment Capital with less than $50 million in AUM at the end of a banner 2009.

That client was well rewarded for staying, as Endowment Capital produced gross returns in excess of 100% for the combined 2008-2009 period with only a modest drawdown in 2008.

With performance back at the top of most databases, Philip tried to renew a marketing effort. He had emerged from the financial crisis with outstanding performance, clear differentiation, and strong business leadership, but he found that his business had been mortally wounded when his dream roster of clients also acted as a single decision investor. He had lost the momentum the business held at launch and was unable to regain the scale needed to make major institutions comfortable. Philip closed the business in early 2014.

Not many hedge fund managers have the experience, relationships, and wherewithal to attract such a prestigious group of clients. Philip likely could have leveraged his initial client base to build a diversified, stable business. But in focusing on a single client type, Endowment Capital Group lived by the sword and died by the sword.

Lesson for Managers

Diversify Your Client Base to Build a Great Business

Great businesses usually have a diversified customer base. A sound investment firm should be no different. While some client types may generally have a longer time horizon than others, broad swaths of investor types are not homogenous entities. An aspirational objective for a manager may be to seek like-minded clients whose allocation decisions are driven by different factors.

Lesson for Allocators

Follow Your Own Voice When Exiting Managers

An allocator's decision to invest in or redeem from a manager is a complex process, so it might be surprising that many outcomes are driven by the single factor of recent performance. Allocators tend to ascribe cause and effect to performance woes, highlighting the known imperfections in a manager exactly when results disappoint. Managers often rebound from the depths of poor performance without changing anything in their portfolios or process. Even when other respected allocators are headed for the exits, each one should think for himself in assessing the prospective outlook for returns.

4

TEAM

People determine success in the start-up phase of an investment business. Start-up hedge funds are small shops, and each team member has a direct impact on the firm's culture and the bottom line. A manager's choices of colleagues and organizational structure are among the most important he will make.

Managers often need to make changes to the team in the early years irrespective of the thoroughness of their planning. Some of these changes come from common mistakes in structure that managers can avoid.

YOUR SINGLE BEST INVESTMENT

"It's all about the people."

—Peter Drucker, management consultant and author

Hedge fund managers are not known for their excellence in managing people. They spend the majority of their time searching for ways to make money and building repeatable processes around winning investment ideas. Most do not devote time and energy to developing their talent and culture.

A manager's single best investment will be the one he makes in his team. Described articulately by Jason Karp, founder of Tourbillon Capital, "if trained properly, people have more duration, more yield, and more optionality than any stock I have ever purchased."[1]

A start-up manager has an opportunity to create a productive culture able to stand the test of time. By building a team aligned with the entrepreneur's mission and reinforcing key principles, a manager can best prepare to execute.

The Imprint Group[2]

Attracting, developing, and retaining a team is easy to say, but requires a great deal of effort to pull off. The Imprint Group ("Imprint") is a boutique talent advisory firm that specializes in helping leading asset management firms sustain growth through a focus on people. Founded by Carol Morley, Neeraj Garg, Dana Galin, Greg Durst, and Sascha Proudlove, Imprint combines deep industry knowledge, strategic thinking, and a rigorous methodology to enable investment leaders and their teams to think bigger and perform better.

Imprint believes that the key to better organizational performance lies in unlocking the value of people. Investment firms that will become future industry leaders will be those that put the right people in the right seats, firing on all cylinders and working more effectively together. In an interview in the spring of 2015, Carol described a looming talent crisis in asset management:

> *The asset management industry is interesting. In spite of talent being so central to success, there is often limited understanding of how to tap people's full potential and create a culture that*

promotes full engagement and top performance. There is tremendous value to be gained by bringing talent management practices in the investment management industry out of the dark ages. ...

Talent development has been a long-standing and proven strategy to create value in other industries—think about industrials, professional services, consumer products—GE, IBM, Price Waterhouse, P&G, Pepsi, to name a few—but it is still a novel concept within the investment arena. ... Compared to many industries, [asset management is] still in adolescence. In particular, alternatives tend to attract young people and adopt a "grow-your-own" mentality. This insular approach to talent has resulted in limited cross-fertilization of best practices from other industries, including talent development.

While perhaps not a visible "burning platform" issue, there is an iceberg looming under the water and we foresee more frequent and more dramatic failures in the future if people issues don't take a front seat.[3]

Highlighting the need for better talent practices in asset management is only a first step in making improvements. Fortunately, Imprint is a few steps ahead of the pack and created the following Top 10 list for managers.

The Imprint Group's Top 10 Success Strategies for Building a High-Performing Team

1. *Know thyself.* Articulate who you are at a deep level—your superpowers, core needs, motivators, values, stumbling blocks, hot buttons, and dial-up opportunities. This knowledge is critical in aligning the firm with who you are, inspiring you, and enabling you to attract the right team.

2. *Make informed choices about your founding team.* Look for people with complementary strengths, thinking styles, experience, and skills, and consider the team dynamics that may evolve. Leverage the science of executive assessment to gain a more informed view of your prospective team members.

3. *Align on vision.* Why does what you do matter? An inspiring view of the future can entice the right people to your organization, and the clearer your vision, the more aligned your team will be in seeing it through.

4. *Create your culture.* Culture, like breathing, will happen automatically whether you think about it or not. Design your culture or watch it develop at your own risk. Clarify the collective values that will govern your firm, put repeatable practices in place, and assign a champion for each.

5. *Define roles, but don't be defined by them.* Throw out the old job description and invite each person to craft a personally inspiring "impact statement." Engender a "one team" mentality among functions to avoid the typical silos that form across the investment, marketing, and operations teams.

6. *Cultivate a "partnership mind-set" throughout the firm.* Encourage every person at the firm to genuinely care about the success of each team member and feel a sense of personal responsibility for making that happen.

7. *Invest in relationship health.* The subtle undercurrents of relationship friction often can be just as damaging as obvious tensions between team members. Help your people thrive by tracking and monitoring the health of their most important relationships with a scorecard. Learn about how unproductive relationship patterns evolve, and create regular forums for your people to connect in meaningful ways as human beings and not just colleagues.

8. *Win hearts, not just minds.* Autonomy, mastery, and purpose are universal motivators, but compensation alone is not.[4] Engage with your people and celebrate wins often so your team feels valued and appreciated.

9. *Develop leaders not just individual producers.* Leadership, like portfolio management, is a blend of science and art and can be taught. Seek out the right experts and actively participate in the process.

10. *Have a talent strategy and put someone in charge of it.* Assign a chief talent officer to the founding partner with the highest emotional intelligence (EQ). In time, consider bringing in a

dedicated chief talent officer. If you wait until you know you need one, you will have waited too long.

In a period of intense focus on doing "stuff," a manager may neglect the vital task of developing the foundation of the firm's culture. A little time, consideration, and expertise can go a long way toward setting a team off in the right direction.

Lesson for Managers

Investing in People Is the Best Decision You Can Make

The hedge fund industry has a void in management and leadership. Managers need to invest more in hiring, onboarding, developing, aligning, and retaining key talent in order to win.

In the early stages of a fund's life, a manager can set a mission, hire a team aligned with that mission, and build processes when the organization is relatively simple. The opportunity cost of churn is high, and managers thinking through team development early in their life will receive high returns on their time.

Lesson for Allocators

Prioritize Talent Development in Your Manager Assessment

Allocators have long checklists that get to the heart of a manager's process, and they spend comparatively little time diving into how managers build and sustain their teams. Understanding a firm's talent strategy should be a key component of an allocator's due diligence process.

THE BEST A MAN CAN GET

> "Managers today have to do more with less, and get better results from limited resources."
>
> —Brian Tracy, author and motivational speaker

Unlike the onetime Gillette razor advertisement describing a perfect shave, "the best a man can get" when launching a start-up investment fund is constrained by the people and financial resources available at the time. A manager must assemble a team, develop a process, and build a culture simultaneously when creating a new fund. Many new firms do not have the financial resources to hire an all-star at every position. Those that do have the budget may find their top candidates happily ensconced elsewhere. New organizations take time to evolve and reach their potential; few get it right out of the box.

Eton Park Capital

Eric Mindich faced both a massive opportunity and a significant challenge when he created Eton Park Capital in 2004. Eric was a known star long before the fund launch. Ten years earlier, at the ripe age of 27, he became the youngest partner ever at Goldman Sachs. A protege of Bob Rubin, he eventually led the trading business to record profits and became one of Goldman's top executives.

The hedge fund industry was primed for a mega launch when Eric decided to leave Goldman. Eric raised a record $3 billion off the bat as allocators thirsted for another high-profile, multi-strategy fund.[5] Amazingly, Eton Park amassed roughly the same amount of assets on day one as Farallon Capital, York Capital, and Och-Ziff Management had scaled into over 15 to 20 years.

Eric believed he had an advantage over legacy businesses. He sought to build a multi-strategy fund from day one that could be excellent in all investment silos, work together to cross-fertilize ideas, and supersize the best opportunities. Armed with the financial resources to acquire high-priced talent, Eric looked for the best people available across strategies and geographies. He sought to build a collaborative culture and aligned each aspect of the operation toward that end.

While putting together a great team on paper, Eric could only hire the talent that was available at the time of his launch. To some extent, he began Eton Park at a competitive disadvantage to peers who had two decades to hire, develop, and retain team members. Within two years, four of the original partners, who did not fit into Eric's vision for the business, had left the firm.[6]

Eton Park proved a success under Eric's leadership and remains a thriving firm managing $8 billion in assets with a successful decade-long track record today. Nevertheless, that outcome was far from a preordained conclusion.

Lesson for Managers

Your Organization Will Evolve, but Your Culture Remains

The challenge of building a nascent team and developing a productive culture is formidable regardless
(Continued)

of the financial situation of the firm. Cohesiveness may be expedited by partnering with former colleagues who have a similar investment approach and communicate with team members in familiar ways. When the launch constitutes a newly formed team, managers improve the odds of success by taking their time to gel and communicate effectively with each other.

Lesson for Allocators

Expect Some Ugliness Inside the Sausage Factory

While academic studies may show that early-stage managers outperform later-stage ones, allocators should have their eyes wide open when new teams come together. It's always ugly inside the sausage factory, even if the ultimate product tastes great.

THE TWO-HEADED PORTFOLIO MANAGER MONSTER

> "Two heads are better than one" (so long as one is slightly smaller than the other).
>
> —Proverb (edited)

A successful hedge fund requires leadership with both business and investment acumen. These different skill sets are not often found in the same person. Start-up partnerships often are well served to have more than one smart head wrapped around the many facets of investing and running a business.

In contrast, a co–portfolio manager construct is a recipe for failure. Gunshot marriages of convenience rarely survive due to egos, differing risk appetites, personnel issues, and a host of other reasons. Sometimes the partnerships work for a while, only to get tested in periods of stress. Better-structured investment organizations have slightly unequal investment leaders, where one portfolio manager drives the car, and the other second-guesses his directions.

Sabretooth Capital[7]

Craig Perry and Erez Kalir were individually among the brightest, most insightful, hardest-working investors I had come across around the time of their launch in 2009. With stellar academic pedigrees; work experience at King Street Capital and Eton Park Capital, respectively; and top-echelon references that spoke about them glowingly, Craig and Erez joined forces to launch Sabretooth

Capital after managing capital under the watchful eye of Julian Robertson. Although they did not have a long history together, Craig and Erez were methodical about both the foundation and structure of their personal partnership, the business, and the investment process. They employed a professional coach to work with them and took great strides to understand each other's strengths and weaknesses.

Sabretooth developed an innovative framework for sourcing investments and structuring the portfolio. Craig and Erez blended a core of event-driven investments with tails of asymmetric hedges to protect against either an inflationary or deflationary environment. The combination of the talent of the principals, a differentiated product, and excellent early performance led to asset growth. By mid-2011, Sabretooth managed $700 million in its flagship fund.

For all of its positives, Sabretooth began to struggle with the co–portfolio manager structure when stresses in Europe in the fall of 2011 hit the capital markets. Seeing problems arising in pockets of overnight lending, Sabretooth came to believe that Europe was on the cusp of a debt crisis that could parallel what the United States experienced in 2008. Both Craig and Erez believed that the European financial system, and its banks in particular, faced a high probability of catastrophic failure. They took bearish positions in the portfolio to protect against the event, while maintaining the integrity of their approach with ballast in event-driven names. Their hypothesis proved incorrect; Europe managed to stave off disaster, creating losses for their portfolio.

Resetting the portfolio framework from a unified directional stance to a normalized construction lacking the excitement of home run potential or the potential for a rapid recovery of recent losses proved too challenging for the partnership to bear. In some instances, Craig and Erez agreed about securities, but did not agree about the timing or sizing of trades. In others, they held divergent views about where to position the fund within their risk management parameters in the face of a drawdown. They could not coalesce on a portfolio framework that made sense in a global stimulus-induced world.

Craig and Erez decided to wind down the partnership in 2012 despite managing over $500 million at the time. Once they came to believe the co-manager structure inhibited their ability to generate superior performance, their only way forward was to return client capital. The pair stayed true to one of their founding principles of putting their clients first.

Algebris Investments[8]

With financial backing and infrastructure support from Chris Hohn of TCI in London, in 2006 Davide Serra and Eric Halet launched Algebris Investors, a global financial services focused hedge fund. As in many hedge fund start-ups with two portfolio managers, Davide and Eric seemed to be a complementary match. Davide, an experienced sell-side analyst at Morgan Stanley, had an incomparably charming personality and deep roots with management teams in the sector. Eric came from a venerable financials team on the buy side at Wellington and took a deeply analytical approach to research. They gathered a talented team of analysts to cover the regions of the world and raised $1 billion in a high-profile launch.

Algebris lived up to its billing right out of the gate. Davide and Eric delivered an eye-popping return of 50% in the fund's first full year. Although the fund tumbled in the financial crisis of 2008, it promptly recovered most of the losses in 2009. That year marked the beginning of Central Bank intervention that drove the stock performance of financials far more than the underlying fundamentals of specific businesses. Throughout 2010 and the first half of 2011, Algebris held its positions and weathered volatile monthly returns without making or losing much overall.

In the last half of 2011, fund losses created stress that began to fracture the viability of the co–portfolio manager model. Long positions in European banks in the third quarter succumbed to macro headwinds and the threat of a eurozone breakup. At a key decision point, Davide and Eric held divergent views about how the future of Europe would affect stock prices. Both believed that the ECB would step in to prevent a collapse of the Euro and the banking system; however, Eric felt their actions may not be sufficient to curtail further declines in share prices, while Davide contended that bank stock prices already reflected that left tail risk. Although they were not aligned in thought, the portfolio performed well through the tumultuous period.

The inability to find a common ground at a key juncture highlighted for both the ineffectiveness of a dual portfolio manager structure. In February 2012, Eric decided to leave Algebris and Davide continued apace. Employing a single portfolio manager construct, Davide developed two new strategies and grew Algebris to $2.5 billion at the end of 2014. After some time off, Eric launched Silvaris Capital, a diversified fund that gave him sole portfolio manager authority and a broader playing field to apply his 20 years of research and investing in financials.

Lesson for Managers

The Two-Headed Portfolio Manager Is Nearly Extinct, So Choose a Structure More Fit to Survive

Aspiring hedge fund managers too often choose a partner as a marriage of convenience. Entrepreneurial ventures are inordinately challenging, and sharing the load with a trusted peer or former colleague is appealing. While two heads certainly can be better than one, the partners should develop a clear articulation of roles and responsibilities, and only one should take the mantle on portfolio decisions. History does not shine brightly on funds attempting to share the investment decision-making role.

Lesson for Allocators

Avoid Marriages of Convenience with a Co–Portfolio Manager Structure

Those considering an investment in a two-headed monster need to be aware of the lessons of history. Very few co-portfolio manager structures have survived the test of time.

When considering a possible exception to the rule, allocators should dive deeply into the decision-making process of the two portfolio managers to understand why their structure might work when so many other similar set-ups have failed.

WHERE DO NICE GUYS FINISH?

"Nice guys finish last."

—Leo Durocher, baseball player and manager

"Nice guys finish first. If you don't know that, you don't know where the finish line is."

—Gary Shandling, comedian

The determination and focus of an experienced investor overseeing a small pool of capital is one of the most desirable characteristics of a start-up hedge fund. All else being equal, a talented manager should produce meaningfully higher returns when managing less capital than he would overseeing a larger pool.

"Nice guys" often are embraced by allocators. In the small, close-knit community of investors, the efficient flow of information puts nice guys in good stead. References corroborate their appeal as colleagues and business leaders, and peers and service providers alike want to see them succeed.

However, some nice guys find their personality conflicts with their ambition. In an effort to create a positive, productive culture that can stand the test of time, these nice guys may find that they give underlings too much rope. Managers should control portfolio decisions and put points on the board in the early years.

Herring Creek Capital[9]

Steve Galbraith is one of the industry's most likeable people. He started his asset management career at Sanford Bernstein and Pzena Investment Management and in 2000 became the investment strategist at Morgan Stanley, succeeding the infamous duo of Byron Wien and Barton Biggs. An eloquent writer and thinker about markets, Steve grew close to many of the industry's leading managers and studied their ways from his seat at Morgan Stanley. In 2004, Lee Ainsle wooed Steve to Maverick Capital to help him oversee the portfolio and business. In 2012, Steve left Maverick to launch Herring Creek Capital.

Steve partnered with a former colleague and hired a high-quality team of young analysts at launch. In the initial months, Steve and his senior partner controlled the investment decisions and the results spoke. Allocators rushed in to underwrite Steve's sterling reputation and the firm's outstanding early results. Herring Creek grew to $500 million in its first year.

The fund's returns stalled not long after. In trying to build a collaborative, positive culture, Steve allowed some of the younger analysts to drive portions of the sourcing and research on names. Although his partner and he ultimately made the investment decisions, it became evident that the performance of their names far surpassed the performance of stocks introduced by other analysts.

Steve realized that after two years of reasonable, albeit not standout, returns, he needed to make changes to give the firm the best chance to succeed. He decided to create more hierarchy in the investment process and made difficult personnel decisions, parting ways with two young analysts, redirecting research efforts of the others, and hiring another senior investment professional. Steve placed the investment decisions back in the hands of those who could deliver best. As of this writing, that process continues, performance has improved, and the future will reveal the fruits of Steve's efforts.

Lesson for Managers

Put Your Destiny in Your Own Hands

An investment entrepreneur often draws on his past experience by mimicking his favorite parts of the investment process and developing his ideal culture. Genuinely nice guys often try to create a harmonious environment. In the cutthroat world of asset management, a nice guy needs to balance a positive culture with a structure that can compete at the highest level. The manager should ensure that investment decisions are made at the top, as allocators to start-ups are typically betting on a single manager or small team.

TURNOVER: DON'T KNOCK IT TILL YOU TRY IT

"If you do not change direction, you may end up where you are heading."

—Lao Tzu, philosopher

A small hedge fund in a resource-constrained environment may not be able to attract the talent it wants at launch. If the business has legs, its leader will have a chance to upgrade the quality of the team. When he takes the bold step of enacting change, he may impact returns positively.

The decision to improve an organization also reveals a lot about the head of the firm. For a person who has demonstrated success in managing money but has not managed people, moving his organization in a positive direction manifests business acumen that is necessary for success.

Ironically, investors almost always perceive staff turnover negatively. In large funds, turnover generally is a sign of problems. Established firms are prosperous businesses that have the wherewithal to attract and retain talent. If an important person leaves, the rationale is rarely positive for the firm. But the pattern recognition of turnover in the small manager space is very different from that most allocators have experienced. As a result, investors usually miss this inflection point and the good returns that may follow.

Farthings Capital[10]

Sebastian Clifton launched Farthings Capital in the spring of 2011 after 12 years focused on the technology, media, and communications sectors as an investment banker and rising star at a hedge fund focused in the sectors. When starting out, Sebastian hired a team of three young analysts in his own image from when he joined his prior firm as a 27-year-old. That image was one in which hard work and good investment ideas could lead to a path of financial success. While that was more than sufficient for Sebastian, it took a few iterations of management experience to learn that most of his employees needed a different touch.

In the fund's first quarter, Farthings got off to a very strong start. Through a combination of Sebastian's library of ideas and a few large positions that worked out well, the fund sufficiently caught the eye of investors to attract $150 million after its first year.

As the firm's initial workaholic pace settled into a more sustainable level, Sebastian began to question the trajectory of one of the analysts he had hired. While inclined to work with the analyst to improve, he recognized early on that a start-up hedge fund has few degrees of freedom. He thought long and hard about the potential negative signaling that analyst turnover may have to the allocator community. In the end, Sebastian decided he needed to risk that negative perception for the positive impact a change could have on the firm. He decided to move on and hire someone with more experience.

Shortly thereafter, Sebastian had a difference of opinion with another analyst about compensation that led him to wonder if that hire was the right long-term cultural fit. Once again, he determined that doing the right thing for the organization trumped attempting to appease perceptions and made a second switch within the first year and a half. When Sebastian determined that the third and final analyst from his initial team would not be a long-term fit for the firm either, he figured it was time to look in the mirror.

With each change, Sebastian had learned lessons about managing people. He noted the mistakes he had made in hiring and how he could improve as a manager in the future. He sought to communicate both the positives and negatives he saw in his analysts' work more regularly, letting them know where they stood and showing them a path to improve.

The personnel changes proved wise ones for the organization despite their risky appearance on the surface. In relatively short order, the muted returns that Farthings generated during 2011 improved significantly, as the new hires enhanced the quality of research and the team gelled. Staff turnover ebbed thereafter, and at the end of 2014, Farthings managed nearly $1 billion in AUM.

Lesson for Managers

Make the Changes You Need to Thrive Irrespective of External Perception

In the early stages of a fund's life, a manager may be more concerned about the external perception of team turnover than the negative internal impact on performance and culture of maintaining the status quo. A manager of a nascent organization needs to be successful as both an investor and leader, and one of the tests of successful leadership is making hard decisions. In the end, a manager must put the very best of himself into his enterprise and follow his instincts to do the right thing for the firm.

Lesson for Allocators

Don't Be Alarmed by Change in a Nascent Organization

Generally accustomed to organizational stability in large hedge funds, allocators do not make it easy for managers to make necessary changes. Allocators get antsy when personnel change occurs, perceiving any turnover as a bad thing.

Those on the outside looking in usually put managers in a penalty box for a period of time to assess the impact of personnel changes. Allocators tend to accept the evolution as a positive development after performance improves, even for a relatively short period of time. In contrast, allocators begin to assimilate cause and effect should performance stall or falter. In either case, the stretch of performance is typically too short to actually determine the impact, but that doesn't stop allocators from trying.

PACING GROWTH

"Adopt the pace of nature: Her secret is patience."

—Ralph Waldo Emerson, author

Managers experiencing early success must wrestle with the tension between waving in assets and developing infrastructure to appropriately handle growth. Most of the time, asset growth is a nonlinear process in which a surge in interest from allocators occurs all at once.

Striking while the iron is hot often makes sense, as business momentum can prove fleeting when prevailing market winds shift. However, too much growth may shrink the investment opportunity set or strain the resources of the team.

Alternatively, slowing the pace of growth to maintain the full integrity of what made the firm successful can be a welcome pause in the eyes of clients. Unfortunately, the same clients and prospects who embrace a business being run "the right way" may quickly turn a blind eye should performance fail to keep up with the previous record. Since no one knows what the future will bring, no right answer for resolving this tension exists.

When a small fund grows to a certain size, it faces a new set of challenges to evolve from a boutique to an institutional organization. Managers turn their attention from the many facets of a start-up to the operations of a business. In growing assets, the manager looks to optimize its mix and foster sustainable relationships that will stand the test of time. As initial kinks in the investment strategy get ironed out, managers focus on refining a repeatable process. They look carefully at the constitution of the team and make changes when needed.

Many managers transition from both a portfolio manager and lead analyst to solely a portfolio manager overseeing a team of analysts. Some make this transition seamlessly, and others struggle in the new seat.

Whether an entrepreneurial fund should make the leap to an institution depends wholly on the desire and capabilities of its leader. Some organizations are well suited to expand, even if incurring some bumps in the road. Others make the conscious decision to stay small.

Lesson for Managers

Stay Connected to the Drivers of Your Success

Hedge funds almost always walk a thin line between rapid growth and protecting the attributes that made it successful. Rarely can a firm dictate its own pace of growth independent of market forces. A manager should understand the risk and rewards involved in difficult decisions about the firm's future and let his instincts lead the way.

Many hedge fund managers have athletic backgrounds, in which coaches played an integral role in their success. Similarly, managers should consider engaging an expert to assist in their leadership

(Continued)

development. Exemplified most famously by Paul Tudor Jones's daily interactions with Tony Robbins for 20 years,[11] industry experts like Randall Stutman at CRA Inc. or Carol Morley at The Imprint Group house a wealth of knowledge that can help take managers to the next level when moving from boutiques to institutions.

Lesson for Allocators

Scrutinize Your Assumptions Regularly When a Firm Grows Quickly

Fast-growing firms require frequent reassessment by allocators. The people, processes, and culture can change before much time passes. Revisiting your investment hypothesis and assumptions is an important exercise to monitor a fast-growing fund.

Sizing up the pace of a firm's growth is a tricky analysis for allocators. From an investment perspective, asset growth necessarily causes a change in the construction of a portfolio, typically compelling a manager to increase the number of positions, keep the same number of positions in larger companies, or keep the same number of positions in similar-sized companies while accepting less liquidity. When

(Continued)

reviewing a hot new investment opportunity, allocators should conduct a cool analysis about the impact of asset growth on future returns.

Rapid asset growth can strain the business as well. Allocators should pay close attention to changes in the firm's hiring practices and culture.

5

INVESTMENT STRATEGY

A manager's investment strategy touches every aspect of his business. The strategy reflects his experience and temperament and is a key driver of the firm's performance. When clearly articulated, the strategy also sets the foundation for the firm's common mission, organization, and marketing story.

FINDING TRUE NORTH

"The customer is always right."

—Marshall Field, entrepreneur

"To thine own self be true."

—William Shakespeare, author

An aspiring hedge fund manager often applies a key lesson from his profession of analyzing businesses and designs his investment strategy to address a perceived need in the market. He speaks to peers, friends, and prospects and receives a cornucopia of advice about his organization, investment process, portfolio structure, and fund terms that others believe he should deliver. In short order, the manager inevitably senses a discrepancy between what he believes the market wants and how he wants to manage capital.

A manager is best served by following his own voice, drawing on his training, experience, risk tolerance, temperament, and instincts to identify the best strategy for him irrespective of demand. When a manager veers away from his true north, he may later find himself stuck in a box ill-suited to match his passion. Managers learn that the many givers of advice intend to help, but they only get in the way of a blissful existence. It's a lot like preparing for a wedding.

At the same time, a new manager faces the reality that doing precisely what he wants may not allow him to attract a critical mass of assets. In the image of Hollywood romances, every manager dreams of finding clients who own their capital, pay little attention to short-term returns, fully understand their investment philosophy and strategy, and leave them alone to focus on investing. Few of these clients exist beyond the confines of friends and family. Many start-ups need to bend their ideals in order to raise money.

Managers ought to consider the long-term consequences of short-term conciliations to prepare the business for success. Allocators tend to recycle capital over time, and whatever decisions a manager makes in the early going to appease investors can have consequences for the future of the business long after those initial investors have departed.

Lesson for Managers

Be True to Yourself

Both in initial planning and through forks in the road, a manager should gather the valued opinion of others as needed and ultimately do what he believes is right. This entrepreneurial venture is his path to take, and he will sleep in the bed he makes.

(Continued)

Lesson for Allocators

Write Down Your Goals in Advance and Make Honest Assessments of Performance Against Those Goals

Allocators should be clear in their hypothesis for investing in a particular strategy and stay true to their intent. While the sophistication of allocators to hedge funds has come a long way in the past decade, all too often clients change their minds based on what worked yesterday instead of holding on to what might work best tomorrow.

Appropriately measuring the value added a manager delivers can be a useful tool to assess what a manager does best. At times, clients can make conscious choices about the strategy and risk profile that best meet their needs through their selection of product offerings.

BEST FOOT FORWARD, WITH BOTH FEET

"The secret of getting ahead is getting started."

—Mark Twain, author

Managers are intensely focused around the first days of their new fund launch. After a period of three to six months setting up the enterprise, hiring a team, meeting potential clients and conducting investment research, the clock finally starts ticking in real time. From day one, investment returns matter.

The market conditions facing a manager out of the gate present an early example of luck playing a role in the success of the business. Start-up funds recognize the importance of performing well in the early months, quarters, and years. Allocators are watching closely, measuring the fund against competitors, and potentially rewarding success through asset growth.

Every new portfolio manager must determine the pace at which he will deploy the initial capital entrusted to him. The choice falls into one of three options:

1. Fully invest the portfolio quickly.
2. Scale into a fully invested portfolio over a month or two.
3. Select best ideas one by one and scale up slowly.

New managers all too often opt for the third option, investing only in their best ideas at launch. Academic research shows that a manager's best ideas outperform all of his ideas,[1] so it seems logical that a manager might want to build a portfolio in which every name epitomizes his strategy. While intellectually satisfying, this approach reduces the probability of success for a new fund.

Scaling into the portfolio slowly gives the new manager more time to complete initial portfolio work, but has the drawback of underinvestment during the period. Presuming that the strategy will make money over time, the resulting cash balance drags down performance. Further, the manager will lag peers at a time when interested prospects are watching closely.

Managers taking this approach may find that perfection can become the enemy of good. By searching for only the best ideas, managers tend to wait for just the right price to add new names to the book. Managers picking names one by one soon find that too much time elapses before the book is fully invested, and the hot prospects that seemed interested at launch fade away.

Getting invested expeditiously almost always is a better path to take. Buying a full portfolio on day one allows a manager to get on even footing with his competitors if market conditions warrant. Given the requisite time managers spend on non-investment matters prior to launch, scaling into the portfolio over a few weeks often is a sensible approach as well. In either case, the sooner a manager gets in the game, the better his chances of competing favorably against peers.

Entrepreneurs usually are chomping at the bit to get started in their new venture and seek to launch their fund as soon as possible. Almost all the time, it behooves a manager to wait an additional month or two prior to launch to build a live portfolio and be better prepared to sprint out of the starting gate.

Estekene Capital[2]

Peter Carlin had high aspirations upon his launch of Estekene Capital. After training as a value-oriented analyst at Sanford Bernstein and spending seven years at long-short fund Alson Capital, Peter struck out on his own alongside former Bernstein and Alson senior analyst Charlie Carr. With backing from a strategic investor, a handful of individuals, and Alson founder Neil Barsky, Estekene got its ducks in a row to launch in March 2010 with close to $100 million in assets.

As thoughtful value investors cognizant of chasing a roaring equity market over the year prior to launch, Peter thought it wise to be methodical in putting on initial risk. He planned to invest slowly and be price sensitive, looking for pockets of opportunity in his favorite ideas to build the book.

Unfortunately, the U.S. equity market didn't cooperate. The Fed-stimulated market continued moving higher throughout Estekene's initial month of March 2010, leaving Peter that much more cautious about adding risk. The Standard & Poor's (S&P) 500 gained 6% in the firm's first month, and Estekene exited March having invested only 10% of its capital. With minimal market exposure, the fund rose 0.6%. Returns were good the rest of the year, but prospects did not easily look under the covers to realize the degree of underperformance that came from the initial month. With ostensibly middling returns in its unadjusted inaugural year, Estekene failed to gain any business momentum.

The firm continued to struggle to put capital to work once it started a step behind. As the market rose through 2010 and the first half of 2011, Estekene remained cautious. After close to two years in business, Estekene had generated strong returns on invested capital and steady, positive alpha, but its high-single-digit annual returns produced no excitement to woo investors into its fund. After three and a half years with minimal asset growth, Peter and Charlie decided to close the partnership.

Lesson for Managers

When Getting Started, Don't Let Perfect Be the Enemy of Good

When preparing to launch a fund, a manager should put his best foot forward, jumping in with both feet. The competition in the hedge fund industry is difficult enough without adding obstacles to performance. Absent prescience calling for a bear market in the strategy, cash balances create a large opportunity cost in the early going. Even if a new fund starts slowly and preserves capital better than others in a tough tape, it must demonstrate the ability to then turn and make money for its clients before prospects will get interested. Getting one market call correct is difficult enough; getting two right consecutively requires twice as much luck.

Lesson for Allocators

Investigate the Quality of a Manager's Early Results—You May Find That Some Babies Are Thrown Out with the Bathwater

In their time-constrained world, allocators tend to get excited about early-stage funds after a period
(Continued)

of high absolute returns. One of the inefficient areas of opportunity for allocators comes from funds that choose to invest initial capital slowly. Since the returns in the early months of these funds may not be representative of steady state for the manager, allocators can blend quantitative metrics with informed questioning to better interpret the potential for a start-up fund.

THE TUG OF WAR BETWEEN FLEXIBILITY AND STYLE DRIFT

"By far the biggest problem for professionals in investing is dealing with career and business risk."

—Jeremy Grantham, investment manager

One of the great advantages of the hedge fund structure relative to traditional vehicles is the breadth of tools a portfolio manager can deploy. Far removed from benchmarks and tracking error, hedge funds can invest long or short, up and down a capital structure, across asset classes and geographies, with concentration or diversification, and in new and innovative areas. The most attractive feature of the investing style to leading managers is the removal of constraints on making money.

However, flexible mandates pose a challenge for allocators. Almost every allocator has a family, client, or investment committee to answer to about their manager decisions. Allocators need to describe expectations for performance in different environments and explain deviations from those expectations. When a client comes across unexpected performance, a drift in strategy, or a change in the team he cannot explain, he may face a formidable challenge reunderwriting his thesis and maintaining the manager's place in the portfolio.

While possessing complete flexibility sounds appealing in theory, every hedge fund manager overseeing capital for others must solve the practical puzzle of how to set expectations. A simple matrix shows the challenge managers face when considering a shift in strategy:

	Right	**Wrong**
Stay the Same	Strategy Works	Stick to Knitting
Evolve	Earn Flexibility	Termination Risk

If a manager sticks to his strategy and implements well, he will earn outsized returns in a good environment and explain away weaker performance in a poor one. As long as the strategy works across a full market cycle, the manager has a good chance to retain his clients.

However, changing a strategy to evolve with the times is a riskier proposition for the manager's business. If his opportunism proves successful straight away, he may earn the right to be flexible for the long term. But if the shift fails to perform in the short term, the manager may lose some clients even if he is ultimately right on the stance. Most clients will call out the manager for style drift and exit.[3] More often than not, managers consciously choose to forgo elements of the flexibility purportedly in their remit in exchange for better odds of sustaining their business for the long term.

Multi-Strategy Hedge Funds

Most multi-strategy hedge funds have been made, not born. Many of the famed alumnae of Bob Rubin's risk arbitrage desk at Goldman Sachs (Tom Steyer, Richard Perry, Daniel Och, Frank Brosens) built hedge funds (Farallon Capital, Perry Capital, Och-Ziff Capital, Taconic Capital, respectively) that began as merger arbitrage pools and later extended to distressed debt investing.[4] Other multi-strategy funds today similarly started with a core expertise from which they extended opportunistically, such as Citadel in convertible bond arbitrage[5] and D. E. Shaw in quantitative investing.[6]

In the early years of my career, hedge funds generally fell into the broad strategy buckets of long-short equity, multi-strategy arbitrage, and macro/CTAs. After stepping away from allocation to attend business school and invest directly from 1997 to 2001, I came back to find that "multi-strategy arbitrage funds" had rebranded themselves as simply "multi-strategy funds."

As assets grew in the early 2000s, demand for multi-strategy arbitrage funds surpassed the supply of opportunities in merger arbitrage and distressed debt investing. In response, the entrepreneurial leaders dynamically adjusted their playbook and broadened their more rigid, pre-espoused strategy. Multi-strategy funds leaned on the credibility earned from a decade of outstanding investment returns to expand into the bigger sandbox of long-short equity. Using similar frameworks for thinking about risk and reward, these managers created the business of hedged special situation investing.

In later years, multi-strategy funds continued to seek new frontiers in adjacent markets requiring comparable skill sets. They exemplify a successful transition from a narrow mandate to a broader one with wider latitude.

Whitebox Advisors[7]

Andrew Redleaf had a rich history in math and options pricing by the time he created Whitebox Advisors in 2000. After earning undergraduate and graduate degrees in math at Yale University, Andy spent 16 years as an options trader. In 1994, he became a founding partner of Deephaven Asset Management, where he managed a convertible arbitrage portfolio. He left Deephaven in 1998 and created Whitebox two years later. Andy chose a firm name that spoke to the antithesis of a "black box" quantitative strategy, signaling his openness in sharing his methods with clients.

Andy wanted Whitebox to be a generalist firm focused on identifying asymmetry across markets. He had developed skill sets through his convertible arbitrage strategy that spanned fundamental equity analysis, downside credit assessment, volatility trading, derivative hedging, and primary market dealing. He wanted the firm to offer a blueprint for how to best deploy these skills across adjacent markets.

In order to avoid the perception that Whitebox would be a convertible arbitrage shop, Andy first offered a statistical arbitrage strategy. He bootstrapped the first fund with $10 million, and after a strong first year, assets grew to $50 million at the beginning of 2001. The firm launched a convertible arbitrage strategy a year later, and performance soared. With firm assets over $200 million, Andy introduced a credit strategy and a multistrategy fund in 2002.

Each of Whitebox's funds came out of the gate with stellar performance that lasted through 2007, positioning the firm to maintain flexibility in its mandates. Prior to the financial crisis, Whitebox noticed a wild asymmetry in the residential mortgage-backed securities market, whose prices were driven in part by a similar embedded option to that in convertible securities. The firm created a special-purpose vehicle to short subprime mortgages and take advantage of a mispricing unlike any it had ever seen. It became one of the few managers that earned a windfall in the collapse of those securities in 2007 and 2008.[8]

Whitebox's core products emphasized credit investments and suffered in the financial crisis despite the profits generated from shorting subprime mortgages. In the aftermath of its performance troubles, the firm leaned on its proclivity to identify exceptional opportunities and created two special purpose vehicles to purchase deeply distressed corporate credit. Those strategies delivered outstanding gains and helped the firm quickly rebuild its asset base.

Today, Whitebox manages $4.5 billion across convertibles, credit, and equity, and has retained the flexibility of a generalist that Andy designed for the organization at its onset. It exemplifies a firm that started with a flexible mandate from day one.

The Survivors in Convertible Arbitrage

While rebranding in the manner of the multi-strategy funds has become more difficult in today's specialized and institutionalized era, the evolution of a handful of convertible arbitrage funds provides a fascinating example of firms in which flexibility trumped style drift.

Convertible arbitrage constituted a core hedge fund strategy in diversified portfolios from the industry's early days. The strategy of buying convertible bonds and hedging with equity shorts allowed leading convertible bond funds to deliver equity-like returns with substantially less risk for many years until the financial crisis hit.

By the time 2008 rolled around, hedge funds and prop desks dominated the convertible market and employed massive amounts of leverage in the process.[9] When the Lehman bankruptcy catalyzed a freezing of credit, convertible bond prices tanked, leverage available to hedge funds dried up, and convertible arbitrage funds experienced massive losses, most of which became permanent as investors withdrew capital and funds closed. Long-time, multibillion-dollar stalwarts, such as Lydian Asset Management and Arbitex Investors, never recovered and ultimately closed their doors.

Most investors gave up on the strategy and never looked back. But in the ensuing years, a curious thing happened. A handful of participants in the space, including Pine River Capital Management[10] and Aristeia Capital,[11] survived the crisis and delivered solid performance. Moreover, they generated returns in the face of headwinds for the core convertible arbitrage strategy, suggesting that something had changed.

The convertible arbitrage funds that survived the crisis evolved their organization beyond a narrow mandate long before the crisis ensued. In the mid-2000s, Aristeia took on quantitative investing and special situation investing, which have remained mainstays of the organization ever since. Pine River introduced a mortgage and fixed-income fund that provided a robust opportunity set through the crisis. Both funds weathered the downturn better than singularly focused competitors by gradually extending beyond a narrow focus on convertible arbitrage.

At the end of 2014, Aristeia managed $4 billion and Pine River $14 billion, and both have generated enviable, risk controlled returns for their investors.

The Winners in the Housing Collapse

Almost every one of the hedge funds that profited by shorting subprime mortgages in 2007 was not a mortgage specialist. Whether in dedicated pools like John Paulson's Paulson & Co. or Whitebox Advisors, or embedded in a multistrategy fund like Baupost Capital, Elliot Management, Passport Capital, or Hayman Capital,[12] the hedge funds that shorted subprime mortgages in a meaningful way in 2006 and 2007 generally were not mortgage insiders. In one of the greatest trades in financial market history, those closest to the action seemed to miss the forest through the trees. Only those who had found a way to engender flexibility outside of a narrow mandate successfully took advantage of the once-in-a-lifetime opportunity.

Scion Capital[13]

In 2001, self-taught investor Dr. Michael Burry left his career in medicine to take up investing full time. He had gained a following from blog posts that led to his acquiring two seed investors for Scion Capital, a long-short equity fund. Michael sought to take unfashionable positions and did his own work. In his first five years, he posted startlingly strong results through contrarian thinking and astute stock picks. Scion more than doubled investors' money during a period when the S&P 500 fell.

Michael identified credit problems in the financial system at large as early as 2003 and had written countless letters to his investors with ominous overtones. In 2005, he bought large positions in credit default swaps to bet against subprime mortgage bonds. Michael's investors were aghast that he had acted on his draconian macro views and moved outside of his proven success picking stocks. The noise from investors grew louder when the subprime position initially created losses in 2005 and 2006.

Unfortunately, Michael faced a challenge far more significant than getting in an investment too early. He had shied away from interpersonal communication throughout his life, and around this time he discovered that he had Asperger's syndrome. Through no fault of his own, Michael simply could not relate well to his investors.

Scion's investors grew disenchanted by Michael's explanation of his contrarian position in securities outside of the fund's equity mandate. A difference of opinion turned into disgruntlement and lawsuits. By the time Scion's investors made substantial profits from the sub-prime short, they were eager to run for the hills. Michael returned most of Scion's capital to investors in 2007 and closed down the firm in 2008.

Michael's story manifests that successful investing is not enough to sustain a business, particularly when deviating from clients' expectations.

Lesson for Managers

Communicate Frequently with Clients to Sustain a Flexible Strategy

Many hedge fund managers thirst to invest with a wide degree of flexibility, yet few navigate the winding road that allows that dream to become a reality. When crafting an initial business plan, start-ups should carefully consider their optimal degree of flexibility over time and pursue an agenda that best suits their skills and interests.

Some managers seek flexibility in their initial mandate, and others evolve their strategy over time. Managers must set expectations with clients from the onset and communicate alterations to the plan regularly. Unexpected surprises cause anxiety among clients.

Lesson for Allocators

Communicate Thoroughly and Openly with Managers to Develop a Shared Understanding of Expectations

Setting expectations is challenging when a mandate calls for flexibility. An allocator should be clear up front about the degree of flexibility he expects from a manager.

Many investment strategies are cyclical, and allocators need to determine in advance whether a particular manager has the dexterity and business acumen to broaden his mandate over time. For those who do, allocators may need patience to rebuff the likely impact of Murphy's Law in the early period when a manager tries something new.

STICK TO YOUR KNITTING

While some funds seek flexibility, others opt to focus narrowly on the strategy, geography, or sector in which they were trained. Managers can create a competitive advantage in their area of expertise by focusing intensely on a single strategy.

Allocators have developed a deeper understanding of the drivers of hedge fund returns. In the past, allocators may have compared hedge fund managers to an amorphous "absolute return" bogey. Today, allocators have customized benchmarks to measure value added relative to market beta (such as equity or credit), hedge fund beta (merger arbitrage or convertible arbitrage premium), sector exposure, geographic exposure, duration, interest rates, and an array of other dependent variables of return.

Underlying risk factors are not always neatly evident in advance. The challenge that arises for managers of focused mandates comes after tough times for their strategy. Diminished returns may lead to the discovery of risk factors not present in a more benign environment. These periods of time can prove very challenging for a nascent hedge fund business.

Edgemont Partners[14]

In December 2002, Ken Guch and Dan Mully launched Edgemont Partners. Both had been well trained in the discipline of investing in idiosyncratic, event-driven special situations. Ken was the first analyst at Och-Ziff Capital Management, and Dan received training at multibillion-dollar Davidson Kempner Capital Management. Edgemont pursued a strategy that embodied their past experience, which stylistically proved a great fit for their skill set and risk tolerance.

Ken and Dan happened to spin out at a propitious time to launch a start-up. The hedge fund industry had delivered steady positive performance when broad market indexes declined in 2000–2002, after which institutions began making significant allocations to hedge funds. At the same time, a host of brand-name, tenured hedge funds closed to new capital, creating an environment where allocators woke up every day wondering where they could find the next hedge fund to meet their portfolio needs. One logical source of new product arose from spin-outs of well-known shops, and Edgemont fit the bill.

Edgemont's investment philosophy and strategy had been drilled into Ken and Dan by their prior employers. They sought to identify special situations (spin-offs, restructurings, mergers, divestitures) and hedge out systematic risks (market, industry, capitalization) with a basket of comparable companies. By isolating the event exposure, Edgemont could express its skepticism of market timing and traditional fundamental long-short investing.

Starting as a bootstrapped fund, Edgemont performed well and quickly attracted interest from allocators. It delivered on its objectives and generated smooth double-digit returns with limited net market exposure, for which a few dozen early adopters plowed into the fund. Just three years after its launch, Edgemont grew its assets under management to over $1.5 billion.

After two great years, returns in the subsequent two years fell to more pedestrian mid-single-digit levels. Edgemont studied its performance attribution and found that a historically anomalous return spread between sectors had created a new set of issues for its hedging strategy. The core of Edgemont's book constituted carefully selected long and short positions, offsetting key risk factors. It then looked at the aggregate level of exposure borne through its bottom-up security selection and generally chose market indexes to offset residual risk. In addressing this residual, Edgemont had a portion of its short book in the Russell 2000.

The performance of the Russell 2000 had a high historical correlation to Edgemont's long book, but the index significantly outperformed in 2005–2006. Upon investigation, Ken and Dan found that certain sectors, notably commodities, energy, and utilities, massively outperformed other sectors of the market. Edgemont's bottom-up security selection in those two years did not yield the proportional amount of long exposure in the anomalously outperforming sectors. The unanticipated sector mismatch interrupted the firm's prior strong and steady returns.

Edgemont considered whether it should alter its strategy or stick to its original game plan. Ken and Dan decided to stay true to its focused mandate, but also seek to add flexibility by introducing a new product. Through analysis of its trading data and insights from allocators, Edgemont created a second fund that incorporated more concentration and reduced residual hedging in order to respond to the changed market environment. Two large investors helped shape this new fund and supported it. In addition, Edgemont addressed the potential for inadvertent sector mismatches in the original product by focusing more precisely on the sector composition of market indexes.

As Murphy's Law would dictate, Edgemont segregated its clients into their preferred use of the firm's skill set and risk habitat just in time for the market's uninterrupted rise to roll over in 2008. Some clients were scarred by the financial crisis and redeemed their investment, but Edgemont continued to stick to its knitting. The firm raised additional capital and had a number of strong years following the crisis.

Lesson for Managers

Anticipate the Inevitable Ebb and Flow of a Focused Strategy

Markets tend to change course on a proven, focused strategy. A manager choosing a narrow mandate should be prepared to weather difficult environments to generate returns.

Without advanced preparation, a manager may be tempted to shift his strategy to cater to changing market winds. A manager needs to carefully assess whether he believes changes in the market are cyclical or secular in nature and proceed accordingly. More often than not, a manager reacting to what worked yesterday gets whipsawed going forward unless he adapts thoughtfully and analytically to evolving market conditions.

Lesson for Allocators

Communicate Thoroughly and Openly with Managers to Develop a Shared Understanding of Expectations (Again)

Similar to the lessons for allocators in flexible strategies, focused strategies have particular drivers that will shine some days and falter in others. An allocator to such strategies should be clear up front about the cyclicality in returns he expects.

An allocator should tear apart the underlying drivers of return and separate those explainable by market conditions from those driven by the skill of the manager when monitoring focused managers. Hedge funds often require an allocator to bundle risk factors together and pay a lot for exposures he might access more cheaply elsewhere. It is incumbent on an allocator to unscramble the mess, identify his investment objectives, and find the best vehicle to execute.

BUILDING BLOCKS OF PROCESS

"We should work on our process, not the outcome of our processes."

—W. Edwards Deming, engineer and author

Every successful hedge fund shares the common attribute of espousing a well-articulated investment philosophy, strategy, and process. Though no two statements of "why, how, and what" are the same, managers without a compass to point to north stand little chance of weathering challenging markets and competing against peers who have embraced a deeper understanding of their place in the investment world.

Surprisingly few small funds espouse deep insights as to why their strategy should work. In his seminal work, David Swensen describes hedge funds as strategies "dedicated to exploiting inefficiencies in pricing marketable securities."[15] A manager competing for capital needs to describe why these inefficiencies exist and why his firm is particularly well suited to exploit them. The absence of a philosophical underpinning for a manager's strategy may result in a loss of discipline and focus when navigating ever-changing market conditions.

With a philosophy to put context around the investment opportunity, a manager turns to his strategy to explain how he will make money. Strategies marry the team, investment process, and portfolio. A sound strategy includes a discussion of risk, reward, and portfolio construction that fits nicely with the team that will implement the strategy.

Diving deeper into the investment process, a manager should articulate its building blocks, including sourcing ideas, conducting research, making investment decisions, managing risk, and reviewing the process for enhancements. Each aspect of the investment process should be easily understood and consistently applied.

Tourbillon Capital[16]

Before founding Tourbillon Capital in 2012, Jason Karp had an unusual breadth of investment experience. Upon graduating from the Wharton School at the University of Pennsylvania, Jason got started in the business as a quantitative analyst, deploying his programming skills toward modeling, quantitative research, portfolio management, and risk measurement. After four years staring at numbers, he grew curious about the companies whose tickers he traded and switched to managing a fundamentally driven portfolio at the same shop. A few years later, Jason took a seat at the top of a large multi-manager hedge fund platform, where he helped create a manager screening and hiring process, oversaw risk, and ran a best ideas portfolio. His final stop before founding Tourbillon was serving as the co–chief investment officer for multi-billion dollar AUM manager Carlson Capital.

When creating his own enterprise, Jason selected the approach best suited to him and was methodical in explaining each element of his strategy. He named the firm after a nineteenth-century invention that reflected his investment philosophy. A tourbillon is the component of a watch that enables its accuracy, a task that proved inordinately challenging for watchmakers before its discovery. Bringing his multidisciplinary experience to the fore, Jason sought to build a repeatable process that could address seemingly uncontrollable markets and random events in the same way a tourbillon brought order to the complex task of telling time.

In order to execute on his philosophy, Jason created a strategy and investment process that drew on the best practices he witnessed at his prior employers. Tourbillon would source ideas using fundamental, quantitative, and behavioral factors. Its research process began with top-down themes, from which it dove into bottom-up research and blended fundamental analysis with an assessment of market expectations. Finally, its portfolio construction combined conviction, trading, and risk management to identify the best way to express ideas.

Tourbillon's opportunistic equity strategy has layers of depth beyond many long-short funds, yet Jason went to great lengths to explain the firm's framework in each aspect of the business. In many areas of the investment process and business, Jason built checklists to turn his insights into repeatable processes. Inspired by Atul Gawande's *the Checklist Manifesto*,[17] these checklists emphasize process over outcomes across the firm, including hiring new team members, team evaluations, sourcing investment ideas, conducting research and due diligence on ideas, portfolio and risk management, trading, and operations. Tourbillon's checklists enabled team members to follow through consistently on much more information than any individual person could be expected to remember in his head.

Within a year of launching Tourbillon, Jason had raised over $1 billion on the back of his articulation of the firm's approach and the resulting outstanding investment performance that suggested proof of concept. Despite a more complex story than many long-short funds, Jason effectively communicated the philosophy, strategy, and process behind Tourbillon's engine, enabling prospective clients to see how the machine would work.

Lesson for Managers

Pay Attention to Process and Outcomes Will Follow

Telling a compelling story about process is a prerequisite for capital raising and investment success. Following the framework of "why" (investment philosophy), "how"

(Continued)

(investment strategy), "what" (investment process), "who" (investment team), "when," and "where" (timing of investment opportunity) creates a sensible outline for a manager to follow.

Lessons for Allocators

Pay Attention to Process and Outcomes Will Follow (a Lesson So Nice It's Worth Stating Twice)

Allocators are accustomed to diving deeply into the elements of a manager's process. An allocator can develop checklists to codify his process and ensure consistency and thoroughness in his due diligence. These checklists can evolve over time, fostering a culture of continuous improvement in an allocator's investment process.

6

INVESTMENT PERFORMANCE

"If you (don't) build it, they (definitely) will (not) come."

—Field of Dreams (edited)

Competition in the performance-driven hedge fund industry is like playing baseball in the major leagues. Outperforming benchmarks, a hallmark of traditional asset management, is not a sufficient condition for success as a hedge fund. Clients hold high expectations for returns, and are willing to pay handsomely for funds that deliver.

Managers can do a lot to structure their firm for success, but assets will not follow unless the fund performs. Returns may be as much a function of the market environment as a manager's particular skill in the early going. Over time, performance is the output of a well-conceived process. Managers who focus too intensely on the outcome at the expense of process may come across unintended consequences.

A SLAVE TO MONTHLY NUMBERS

"Patience is a virtue."

—William Langland, poet

In response to client requests, hedge funds report performance far too frequently. In my early days in the business, many funds reported to clients quarterly, some monthly, and none more frequently than that. Today, quarterly reporting is unheard of, monthly is standard, and many funds report weekly or even daily returns. Short-termism has perniciously pervaded the allocation game just as it has invaded corporations through quarterly earnings reports.[1]

George Soros' theory of reflexivity applies to hedge funds in unhealthy ways. By explaining his investment results to clients over short periods of time, a manager may perceive that his clients' time horizon is commensurately short. He meets with clients regularly, during which time they discuss recent activity. The repeated process of these discussions can lead a manager to believe that his clients care about short-term results.

Long-term success cannot come from short-term investment decisions. A manager must stay true to his strategy and understand that communicating with clients frequently can change his investment behavior.

Tiedemann Emerging Markets Fund[2]

Steve Diamond invested around the world in value-oriented situations off the radar screen from index-driven emerging market equity investors and benefited from some of the best training available in emerging markets.[3] He launched an emerging markets equity fund under the Tiedemann umbrella in 2000.

Steve's initial trading strategy focused on delivering monthly returns. He had methodically broken down how he sought to make mid-20% annual rates of return by saying, "If we can make 10 basis points a day, that's 50 a week, and 2% each month. That's all we need to do." In the early days, Steve focused his team's trading on optimizing to that equation. In order to measure the faithful execution of this trading plan, Steve's team essentially cut losers and rode winners on a daily basis.[4]

While a valid trading strategy for some managers, the momentum-driven trading that resulted from a focus on monthly performance was diametrically opposed to Steve's value-oriented investment beliefs. Making money through fundamental research on less discovered emerging-market companies is a strategy that takes time to play out. Steve believed that a falling stock, absent changes to fundamentals, was a better value. His traders, who focused on clipping 10 basis points a day, would sell falling positions instead.

Steve abandoned his daily performance goals once he recognized that his benign attempt to create yardsticks for his team to measure performance had the unintended consequence of inhibiting his investment strategy. For many years until retiring in 2012, Steve experienced great success, at one point growing the fund to $1.7 billion in assets.

Lesson for Managers

Focusing on the Short Term Is Antithetical to Achieving Long-Term Success

Managers should practice mental accounting to segregate their conversations with clients from their investment thought process. This mental framework proves important when short-term returns inevitably lack perfection. Markets have a funny way of inflicting the most pain, on most of the participants, most of the time, and the harder managers push to achieve short-term results, the more markets may punish their efforts.

Managers should understand that a client's question may arise from a different purpose than an interest in short-term performance. A manager stands the best chance of success by keeping his thoughts away from the vicissitudes of short-term performance.

Lesson for Allocators

Your Interactions May Affect Your Manager's Behavior

Allocators need to walk the line between accessing sufficient information to make good investment

(Continued)

133

decisions and encouraging managers to maintain a long-term perspective. When discussing short-term performance or requesting information that might put a manager on the defensive, allocators should clearly communicate their objectives and leave no room for managers to make assumptions.

SUSTAINING PERFORMANCE

"When you reach the top, that's when the climb begins."

—Michael Caine, actor

Managers without a brand name can attract allocators' attention through eye-popping performance. Without stellar performance, it often is quite difficult for a manager to get a lot of traction raising assets.

However, high returns usually go hand-in-hand with a high degree of risk. Whether arising from intelligently selected risks or dumb luck, a manager can post returns that compel prospects to take a look at the fund. If the manager has a good story in hand to explain the results, he stands a reasonable chance of attracting assets.

A manager who raises money off of high returns faces the challenge of continuing to perform at that level.

He must be on the right tail of the distribution twice in a row in order to meet the expectations of clients that witnessed stellar performance. Without continued strong performance, the manager may find that assets fly out the door just as quickly as they came in.

Stoneham Capital[5]

Derek Abruzzese launched Stoneham Capital in December 2002 after a successful career as an analyst and portfolio manager at Soros Fund Management. Derek invested in a very concentrated portfolio of typically no more than 20 total long and short positions in large-cap European companies, believing that he rarely would have more than 20 good ideas at any given time. Explaining his embracing of risk, Derek told clients that when he held conviction in an out-of-favor name, his mantra would be "when in trouble, double."

After a Murphy's Law–like first month, when Derek incorrectly went all-in believing that stocks typically rise in the last month of the year, Stoneham posted three consecutive years of exceptional results. The period reached an apex in April 2006, ending a string of eight straight positive months in which the fund earned 75%. Investors began to take notice of the fund. Holding court near the

New Hampshire border to more than 60 due diligence processes during 2006, assets climbed to a peak of $1.1 billion in June 2007.

While staying true to its concentrated, risk-taking strategy, the tide turned on Stoneham almost immediately after crossing the billion-dollar plateau. Derek started a losing streak in July 2007 that spanned 9 of the next 10 months. The more he was down, the more he stretched to recapture losses. He doubled down on out-of-favor financial stocks in mid-2007 and took a further drubbing. Investors understood that Stoneham's returns would be volatile, but nevertheless lost confidence in Derek after the drawdown. Just over a year after achieving its peak asset level, Stoneham was no more.

Lesson for Managers

When You Think You Have Arrived, Your Next Adventure Will Have Just Begun

In a competitive field to raise capital, some managers go out on the risk curve to demonstrate better outcomes. When this works, allocators implicitly assume the success will continue apace on their money, even if a rational assessment would indicate that mean reversion could occur. Once success has put a manager in business, he needs to continue to produce excellent results in order to stay in business.

Lesson for Allocators

You Will Chase Performance, So Make Sure It Is for the Right Reasons

Funds that stand out for outsized gains are often the envy of allocators feeling an error of omission. Performance chasing occurs in spite of an allocator's awareness of it because high performers provide tangible evidence of the results he seeks. Sometimes his work leads to a belief that the strong results can be expected to persist, and he chooses to proceed despite having missed out of late.

Other times, an allocator concludes that the drivers of return are a function of risk taking in the right place at the right time. In today's marketplace, the risky portfolios that have generated outsized returns tend to fall in the activist camp. Some high-flying managers are likely to stand the test of time, but others may find their fortunes reverse in a less forgiving market environment. These are not poor investments per se, but each allocator should fully comprehend the possible distribution of returns these funds may encounter.

REACHING FOR RETURN

"What the wise man does in the beginning, the fool does in the end."

—Howard Marks, investment manager

Early-stage managers do everything in their power to achieve great results out of the box. Allocators are attracted to this intense period of commitment and focus in a manager's life cycle, which occurs when he is not encumbered by too many assets to manage.

In the process of putting his best foot forward, a small manager occasionally makes the mistake of investing in private equities or similarly illiquid opportunities. On the face, a manager may find a compelling risk-reward that he expects will more than compensate for the illiquidity of the position. However, when taken in the context of the manager's flowing pool of capital, the investment proposition rarely makes sense.

When taking on a private equity position, the manager risks a known percentage of his assets at the time he takes the position. He also has aspirations to grow the firm's capital base over the investment period of the position. If successful in both asset raising and the private investment, the manager will find that his reward is far less than he anticipated when putting on the position.

For example, a manager might put 1% of his fund in a private equity that he expects has a 10× payoff per dollar of downside. In a static portfolio, the position size and potential payoff may justify the trade-off for illiquidity. However, if the original 1% totaled $1 million of a $100 million fund, and three years later, he realizes $10 million after growing the fund to $500 million, the return on the fund will only be 2% (10× a now 0.20% position). While beneficial to fund returns, it's less clear that the upside case of a 2× payout over three years was worth the illiquidity risk.

In any other scenario the private position will pose a challenge for the manager. If the private is successful but the fund remains small, the manager will spend a disproportionate amount of his marketing time explaining the situation. Even worse, if the private is unsuccessful and the fund remains small, future investors will balk at entering the potentially troubling situation. Finally, if the private falters while the fund grows, the manager will get a smaller slap on the wrist and clients may demand that he never dabbles in privates again. No matter how a manager cuts it, small funds are not well situated to make private investments.

Dubuque Capital[6]

In 2005, Ray Kinsella, Terence Mann, and Archie Graham launched Dubuque Capital, a long-short, distressed and special situations fund, after working together in research at a large hedge fund. With Ray managing the portfolio and Terence and Archie scouring for ideas, the team made a series of shrewd investments that led to strong results, including shorting mortgage companies in 2007 and 2008. In the summer of 2009 with assets approaching $100 million for the first time, they hired a first-rate marketer and prepared to tell their story to the investment world.

In 2007, Terrance sourced a seemingly compelling one-off private deal. For the price of $1 million, the fund could take over a partially built apartment complex with an abutting park. Its previous owner had run out of cash after plowing over $20 million of equity into the project. Dubuque expected that it would need to fund $2 million to $4 million of additional capital expenditures over two years, after which the facility could begin enlisting tenants. Dubuque looked at the investment through its distressed lens and believed it had a unique opportunity to make an outstanding return for the fund with low risk.

Through the first half of 2009, Dubuque had outperformed the overall stock market by almost 140%

from inception, but the remainder of the year and the beginning of 2010 were a challenging period for the portfolio. Running close to neutral exposure, Dubuque did not participate in the soaring bull markets and flat-lined in the back half of 2009. A few mistakes on the short side hurt returns in the first half of 2010.

Meanwhile, the apartment complex never turned cash flow positive, and Dubuque continued to fund its operating losses in order to keep it alive. Each time the project was slated to turn the corner, another obstacle came in its path. The time to profitability got pushed back by low rent rolls, delayed permitting, and a new set of tax ordinances in the town. Dubuque invested several million dollars in the business beyond its initial expectations, bringing it to a 7% position after a 2009 write-down, and both Terrance and Archie began spending two days each week at the facility dealing with a host of unexpected issues.

By early 2010, Dubluque had maxed out its private equity allocation at 10% of the fund. At that size, the single investment overshadowed Dubuque's otherwise good returns. Potential investors in the fund saw an eyesore in the private and balked at entering. In light of the disappointing performance in the first half of 2010, the three partners saw no way out of the predicament and decided to shut down the fund in the summer of 2010.

Direct Lending in 2007–2008

In the run-up to the financial crisis, a number of well-regarded distressed debt funds looked for creative ways to augment returns from the low yields available on junk bonds. One innovative tactic was a new business called rescue funding (later renamed the more euphemistic "direct lending"). Rather than compete in the primary market, hedge funds started sourcing corporate borrowers on their own to lend directly. The investment strategy ranged from creating loans that would later refinance or securitize to a "loan-to-own" strategy should the business default.

Direct lending in 2006 had a flawed premise that led to disastrous consequences when 2008 rolled around. In 2006, credit markets were wide open for borrowers. With poor underwriting standards, almost any company could find financing. As a result, hedge funds that lent money to companies in dire straits needed to ask the question of how they would exit a loan to a company that no one else would touch during one of the great bull markets for credit. With the possible exception of loan-to-own strategies, these direct loans most likely would never get repaid at par.

Managers that stretched for yield through direct lending were compelled to freeze redemptions at the end of 2008. The direct loans had no bid in the fall of 2008, and managers had no clearing price to mark their portfolio.

Lesson for Managers

If You Fly Close to the Sun, You're Apt to Get Burned

Managers should steer clear of private investments in the early stages of their fund's life. The math simply doesn't add up, and the positions inevitably result in a poor time allocation for the manager.

Small managers who come across attractive private opportunities should "just say no." Without establishing credibility among allocators and building a sustainable franchise, the unfavorable risk-reward of a private is too much risk for a small fund to bear.

Lesson for Allocators

Focus on What Matters Most

Focusing on what matters most can help allocators create sensible rules to follow. All too often, allocators impose artificial constraints on their investment universe to the detriment of their investment results.

For example, the liquidity of a manager's underlying holdings will ultimately determine the ease with which an allocator can exit. So long as the manager's positions are liquid, an allocator can easily exit a fund without incurring additional losses.

THE ROLE OF LUCK

> "Only two types of hedge funds succeed: those that are lucky and those that are lucky and good."
>
> —Randy Cohen, senior lecturer, MIT Sloan School of Management

One of the great challenges of starting a new investment fund is the self-fulfilling nature of investment returns. Successful hedge fund start-ups experience a virtuous cycle that comes in part from good luck. A fund's short-term performance is often attributable in large part to the beta tailwinds of underlying markets or strategies. With strong initial performance, asset growth is more likely to follow. This asset growth, in turn, can create a positive feedback loop, allowing the manager to hire more and better people to improve his organization. A positive psychological state is both conducive to and essential for continued performance, which in turn leads to further AUM growth and resources to build a better business.

Bad luck can make the cycle work in reverse. When even a very good manager launches into headwinds, weak short-term performance may create challenges in accumulating a critical mass of assets. At times, a difficult stretch of performance can shake the confidence of the best of them, and the cycle may turn to a vicious one.

For an allocator, herein lies the opportunity. The ability to segregate luck from skill, particularly in the early going, leaves a bifurcated marketplace that may not be separated for the right reasons.

Postcrisis Distressed Residential Mortgage Funds

Residential mortgage-backed securities (RMBS) funds have had a rocky history over the past two decades, with fortunes correlating with the U.S. interest rate cycle. In the late 1980s and early 1990s, a handful of funds experienced great success monetizing mispricings in the embedded prepayment option of RMBS products. When the Fed hiked rates six times in 1994, these mortgage funds fell on hard times.[7] After that dislocation, new funds like

Ellington Capital arose and had a few years of monstrous returns until Long-Term Capital Management imploded in 1998, bringing RMBS and most other spread-based strategies down with it.[8]

Following the most recent financial crisis in 2008, a number of new hedge funds arose with teams composed of former proprietary traders at Wall Street banks. LibreMax Capital and Seer Capital, led by alumnae from Deutsche Bank; Axonic Capital and Tilden Park Capital out of Goldman Sachs; and One William Street from Lehman Brothers all launched around 2009. At the time, the entire RMBS sector was out of favor and trading at deeply distressed prices. These firms opened their doors, put one foot in front of the other, and posted outstanding returns. By the end of 2014, each of these new firms managed in the vicinity of $2 billion.

The serendipitous timing of these fund launches allowed every one of them to post among the best returns in the hedge fund industry. It remains to be seen how well these firms will weather a reversal in the interest rate cycle, as history would suggest they will not all survive. In the meantime, the sector as a whole provides an example of the importance of early returns in the successful launch of a hedge fund business.

Senator Investment Group[9]

In a short period of time, Alex Klabin and Doug Silverman demonstrated what can happen when a manager is both lucky and good. Alex and Doug both graduated from Princeton University and started their careers as investment bankers. In 2003, they met at York Capital Management, a multibillion-dollar, global, event-driven investment firm. The pair worked together for five years at York, learning the discipline of value and event-driven investing across global equity and credit markets. They left York in February 2008 with entrepreneurial aspirations to build their own firm. Despite their impressive resumes, neither was known to the allocator community, so they entered into a strategic relationship with a seeder. Alex and Doug launched Senator in July 2008 with $200 million, mostly from the strategic investor.

Some of the exceptional volatility that would later go down in the annals of financial history started wreaking havoc on the markets around the time of their launch. Senator's defensive positioning—long the equity of pasta, soup, and cereal manufacturers and short the credit of highly levered financial institutions—helped them preserve capital when Lehman Brothers failed that September. Despite finishing the year with a slight profit, Senator had not raised much capital beyond its initial investors.

Alex and Doug made another fortuitous timing decision in early 2009 to expand Senator's portfolio to a normalized risk level and capitalize on the once-in-a-lifetime dislocations that existed in both the credit and equity markets. Senator posted positive results in every month of 2009. Investors rushed in the door after seeing Senator protect capital in 2008 and pivot to produce a 60% net return in 2009. Senator grew to $1.5 billion by January 2010.

Some combination of skill and luck set Senator off on the right foot, and prowess kept them going. Over the five years that followed, Senator generated consistent performance above industry averages, making money for the wave of clients that followed the exceptional 2009. Senator has continued to build on its initial momentum for seven years running. Through a combination of strong performance and measured inflows, the firm has grown every year since its launch and managed nearly $9 billion in assets at the end of 2014.

Lesson for Managers

Never Underestimate the Role of Luck

Luck plays an important role in successful outcomes in both investment management and in life. Had the Fed not staved off the financial crisis and taken down Wall Street proprietary trading, mortgage traders would not have had the opportunity to launch new funds in an environment with an abundant supply of distressed paper. Had Senator started a year or two earlier, it may have been fully invested into the financial crisis or, alternatively, may have been underinvested in periods when other managers performed well.

Luck is what happens when preparation meets opportunity.[10] Each of the RMBS managers and Senator spent their careers prior to launch focusing on the elements of success within their control. They were fully prepared to capture the luck that markets afforded them.

Lesson for Allocators

Recognize the Difference between Skill and Luck

Allocators should be keenly aware of the return drivers behind a fund or strategy's performance.
(Continued)

Postcrisis mortgage funds all worked because a market dislocation presented a broad opportunity to buy cheap mortgage securities. Similarly, activist strategies, a hotbed of activity in 2013 and 2014, benefited from a pronounced U.S. equity long bias. Allocators should consider the ramifications of changing market conditions on the underlying strategies they pursue.

THE BEST MONTH IN A MANAGER'S CAREER

> "Anything that can go wrong will go wrong."
>
> —Murphy's Law

For every example of tailwinds like those benefiting RMBS fund launches in 2009, many more times a surge in interest for a fund or strategy follows a period of terrific performance and leads a softer patch. Market conditions are never as easy in real-time as a start-up manager perceives they will be in advance.

The best performance month in a manager's career inevitably comes the month before his launch. There's no reason why this happens, but it seems to occur with alarming frequency.

Signpost Capital[11]

The months preceding the launch of Signpost Capital in early 2012 were exciting ones for portfolio manager Siddharth Thacker. Following his graduation from Harvard Business School, Siddharth worked at Ziff Brothers Investments for five years, where he met each of his three founding partners of Signpost. Though each partner left ZBI at a different time, the quartet re-formed under the umbrella of Citadel's Pioneer Path and worked together for a few years. After significant planning, the group decided to set out on their own and left Citadel in 2011.

Signpost's story resonated with many. Its global long-short focus, employing a long-term horizon, differentiated sourcing of ideas, and diligent research process harnessing lessons from history, led to a portfolio of ideas that didn't look like other funds. Through prelaunch marketing efforts, Siddharth got comfortable that the firm would achieve a critical mass of assets in its initial months, and he turned the team's efforts toward building the portfolio in the fourth quarter of 2011 to prepare to invest fully upon launch.

Signpost was ready to roll with its paper portfolio as the holiday season came around. However, Siddharth began to sense that investors interested in its Founder's Share Class were not planning to sit around during the holidays signing subscription documents, so he made the decision to push off the launch by a month.

As Murphy's Law would dictate, Signpost's paper portfolio posted a return of approximately 6% in the month of January 2012. Rather than launch with a splash, which no doubt would have garnished even more investor excitement, Signpost was left scurrying to refresh the portfolio after a number of its core names reached price targets in just one month.

Signpost performed well enough during the rest of the year to attract a few hundred million dollars, but it never had the chance to post what may have been its best month in January 2012.

7

SO YOU WANT TO INVEST IN A START-UP HEDGE FUND?

Institutions have increased allocations to large hedge funds since the global financial crisis in an effort to protect portfolios dominated by long only risk assets. More recently, these institutions have expanded their horizons within their hedge fund portfolios to better optimize outcomes.

Small managers afford institutions the chance to earn high risk-adjusted returns and meet important spending needs. The dispersion of returns across small funds is much wider than in large funds, providing allocators with ample opportunity to add value through astute manager selection. At the same time, the allocation of capital to talent is inefficient; some outstanding managers are scooped up by investors while other equally skilled ones go undiscovered.

Allocating to small funds can be quite different from investing in large ones. The drivers of success and risk factors vary across stages of a fund's life. Allocators accustomed to investing in brand name funds should allow sufficient time to ascend a learning curve in the small manager space.

INFLUENCING OUTCOMES

"Do unto others what you would have them do unto you."

—The Golden Rule

Competition has increased among allocators to identify the best funds. At times, limited capacity in a small fund gets surpassed by demand, allowing a manager to pick his partners. Allocators can influence their access to desired funds by establishing a positive pattern of behavior.

The way an allocator communicates and the actions he takes can enhance his reputation as an investor. Allocators can start by understanding that they are not special or unique in the eyes of a manager. In *The Four Agreements*, Don Miguel Ruiz describes this universal truth:

> *All people live in their own dream, in their own mind; they are in a completely different world from the one we live in.*[1]

By relating to a manager from a place of humility, an allocator naturally ingratiates himself to a manager. He accomplishes this by optimizing his face-to-face time, carrying a respectful tone, handling bad news gracefully, and terminating managers with dignity.

First, he should be respectful of a manager's time. By preparing thoroughly for meetings in advance, an allocator can spend time with a manager asking better questions and getting deeper into the manager's story. Preparation is common sense, but not common practice. As a result, allocators stand out by doing this simple thing right.

Second, an allocator's tone and demeanor can change the nature of a conversation. The personalities of allocators tend to come out quickly in meetings with managers. Those allocators who choose to ask questions respectfully tend to access information more readily than those constantly on the attack.

Third, allocators show their colors through the delivery of difficult messages. When declining meetings or passing on an opportunity, allocators should follow up consistently, even when the answer is "no, thank you." This common courtesy appears not to be the norm in the industry. Managers would rather know where they stand than being left in the ether.

Similarly, exiting a relationship gracefully can go a long way in building a reputation as a desired investor. Allocators make mistakes, just as their managers do. When an allocator lays out his rationale to a manager and recognizes he may be wrong, he takes ownership over the investment decision and may soften the personal blow to the manager.

Allocators should view their interactions with managers as a continuous evaluation of their character. Those who choose to be on their best behavior may be rewarded down the road.

Lesson for Managers

Mirror Your Potential Partner to Learn Who He Is

In face-to-face meetings, managers can learn a lot about allocators by mirroring their questions and statements back to them. An effective mirror can reflect the truth and help a manager size up his potential partner.

Lesson for Allocators

Be Your Best Self in Your Relationships with Managers

Managers prefer to have supportive partners who are respectful of their priorities, take the time to understand their strategy, ask thoughtful questions, and offer honest feedback in a courteous way. Allocators who follow suit can build a reputation as a desirable investor. In a small world and even smaller community of asset managers, each of our words, behaviors, and actions are interconnected and have the ability to influence current and future relationships.

TERMS

> "If you don't like something, change it. If you can't change it, change your attitude."
>
> —Maya Angelou, author

Allocators are never more excited about an investment in a manager than the day they wire funds. After spending days in meetings, weeks on references, and months on research, an allocator sees stars in his eyes when he commits funds to a new relationship. This dynamic is compounded when investing in an early-stage manager, where the allocator hopes to have discovered the next rising star before others.

Alongside this enthusiasm to get going, allocators to early-stage funds have an opportunity to construct favorable terms. Thoughtful negotiation can lead to a win-win between managers and allocators.

Fees

Whether through a seed arrangement, founder's shares, or other circumstance when capital is scarce for a fund, an allocator can meaningfully reduce his fee burden with a manager. A sensible arrangement might include ratcheting down fees as the fund grows, as the tenure of the relationships ages, or both. Allocators can get rewarded for patience, and managers can increase the stability of their capital base.

Expenses

The fine print of a hedge fund offering memorandum rarely pulls the reins tight on a manager's checkbook. In addition to a hefty management fee relative to traditional funds, hedge fund legal documents often grant a manager broad rights to expense a laundry list of items that allocators might otherwise assume get covered by the management fee. Some are understood and accepted by allocators, such as the compensation of portfolio managers in large, multimanager platforms. Others are smaller in dollars and might appear like nickel-and-diming to unsuspecting investors, such as office rent, research-related travel, subscriptions, and marketing expenses.[2] Early-stage investors have an opportunity to exert influence over the fund terms for the benefit of all future investors.

Transparency

Allocators frequently assume that investing in small funds is riskier than investing in big ones. While small funds do experience more business risk and the potential for unhealthy stress on the manager, allocators can mitigate the direct investment risk by acquiring more portfolio transparency. By blending transparency with vigilant risk management, allocators have access to more information and may reduce the investment risk relative to a more opaque investment in a larger fund.

Liquidity

Allocators also may mischaracterize downside risk when investing in small funds. Whether imposed by a board or by the lack of comfort standing alone, allocators frequently set limits on the proportion of a manager's capital it can comprise. This mechanism is flawed.

Rather than artificially imposing the same constraint on all funds, allocators should consider the underlying liquidity of the manager's investments. So long as a manager can sell positions without incurring market impact, such as in a liquid long-short equity strategy, an allocator need not be concerned about holding a specified maximum percentage of the manager's assets.

A Hole-y Gate

Dating back to the fall of Long-Term Capital Management (LTCM) in 1998, a number of hedge funds created liquidity terms that would prevent a rush of investors for the exit at the exact same time. In 1998, not only did managers facing redemption pressure have to sell positions at an inopportune time, but also managers who thought they might have redemptions were frozen in their tracks. Historically wide spreads began narrowing shortly after these pressures abated, and those with strong hands reaped the greatest rewards. In response, managers sought to limit the amount of redemptions that could occur at the same time in order to prevent an exodus in the future.

The gates created in the ensuing decade came home to roost in 2008, when investors sought liquidity at the height of the financial crisis. Many managers imposed their gates, enabling those funds to hold positions that later bounced back in 2009.

The course of action served its intended purpose, but encountered a series of unintended consequences. First, allocators who suffered the largest losses in 2008 from having invested the highest proportion of their capital in credit strategies (the source of most of the gating) and who barked the loudest at their managers to allow redemptions ironically were rewarded the most the following year when the credit markets soared. Left to their own devices, these allocators may have been a lot worse off.

Second, many large funds with proportionately small individual clients imposed gates, while most small funds with large clients investing in liquid assets allowed capital to leave gracefully. It turned out that owning 1% of a large fund with a gate posed a greater restriction on an allocator's liquidity than owning 90% of a small fund without one.

Third, allocators responded to their distaste for aggregate gates (applied at the fund level) by embracing individual investor-level gates, where each investor must stage the receipt of his withdrawal regardless of exit timing. Investor-level gates have the benefit of clearly defining the mechanism for withdrawal, preventing allocators from playing games and submitting unnecessarily large withdrawal requests.

Investor-level gates leave something to be desired. In theory, an allocator should be comfortable locking up his capital in the early years, as he is never more excited for his relationship with a new manager than when he first invests. The contrary is also true; whether 3, 5, or

10 years later, an allocator may change his mind. When that time comes, it seems perverse that a long-standing client needs to wait a full year or more to access his capital. That is exactly what an investor-level gate creates.

As price makers, allocators have an opportunity to set liquidity terms that best align their interests with those of managers. Aggregate gates with investor-level unwinding mechanisms are better deliveries of a common goal than today's standard investor-level gate.

Lesson for Managers

Strive to Give More for Less

Start-up managers typically turn to hedge fund lawyers to structure the terms of their fund according to normal industry practice. This has led to a current industry state in which allocators believe fees are too high, transparency is too limited, and liquidity is less than desired.

The industry is slowly shifting its terms back toward the wishes of its customers. Managers constructing new funds can get ahead of this trend by considering what might work best for prospective investors and proactively leading their legal advisers

(Continued)

down a better path. When seeking to win business, striving to offer more for less is a worthy goal.

Lesson for Allocators

Look to Start-Ups to Extract Better Terms without Adverse Selection

Early-stage investing allows allocators to access promising talent and set fair terms for the betterment of their investment, the manager's business, and the industry at large. Fees, expenses, transparency, and liquidity are all on the table.

PREPARING FOR BUMPS IN THE ROAD

> "A man must be big enough to admit his mistakes, smart enough to profit from them, and strong enough to correct them."
>
> —John C. Maxwell, leadership author and speaker

An allocator should be prepared to think differently about sourcing, due diligence, decision making, and managing upwards when he decides to play in the small manager arena.

In sourcing, an allocator can level the playing field by sticking to strategies that fall squarely in his zone of competence. Warren Buffett compared investing to Ted Williams' approach to hitting a baseball, saying "waiting for the fat pitch would mean a trip to the Hall of Fame; swinging indiscriminately would mean a ticket to the minors."[3] An allocator should endeavor to see a lot of pitches from small mangers before deciding when to swing.

In the due diligence process, experienced allocators to small funds lean on their qualitative assessment of a manager's character. Building a broad and deep network of relationships is essential to learn about the personalities involved in a new fund.

Allocators should be wary of "story fund investing," the allocator parallel to "story stock investing" by a manager. Story stocks leave a manager ill-prepared to weather volatility and vulnerable to sell at the wrong time. Similarly, allocators gossip regularly about undiscovered funds. Many stories sound sexy and offer the dream that an allocator has identified the next great manager. Allocators need to form independent opinions about the manager's investment philosophy, strategy, process, implementation, and team dynamics. An allocator may be poorly situated to weather inevitable bumps in the road without doing his own work.

Story fund investing is particularly fraught with risk when it leads an allocator to swing outside of his strike zone. Allocators may be lured to an undiscovered manager in a new strategy without the requisite tools to conduct a deep analysis of the investment opportunity.

Finally, allocators need to articulate the intention and expectations of their small fund investments and ensure that their governance structure is prepared to withstand mistakes. By investing predominantly in diversified, large brand name funds, most boards are shielded from the ups and downs of returns below the smooth surface of a multi-strategy line item. To some governance boards, a negative line item may be interpreted as a scarlet letter instead of as a normal part of the investment program. Repeated communication about the process will enable the allocator to stay the course.

Lesson for Managers

Be Frank About the Challenges You Face— Teaching Something of Value May Pay Dividends down the Road

Managers should take the opportunity to educate investors about the benefits and drawbacks of running a small firm. Giving information in the service of others has a nice way of coming around full circle in life.

Lesson for Allocators

Adjust Your Mental Model for the Particular Circumstances at Hand

The assessment, governance, and monitoring of small managers requires its own variation on the theme of investing in large hedge funds. Allocators should adjust their process and mind-set accordingly.

HEED THE STOP SIGN

> "When you come to a fork in the road, take it."
>
> —Yogi Berra, baseball player and manager

Perhaps the most challenging component of an allocator's decision on a rising star is navigating the competitive landscape. No allocator sits in a vacuum, and by definition, a hedge fund's ascension is tied to demand from a number of allocators at the same time.

The fervor in the allocator community can become palpable when a manager announces it will close to new investors. This wave of interest by allocators often hits a manager shortly after he has overearned his long-term objectives. Even when a manager is upfront about this and attempts to temper expectations, an allocator may face a tricky choice between knowingly investing in the manager at a suboptimal time and eschewing the opportunity for good.

Occasionally, a manager feels sufficiently aghast at the soaring interest in his fund that he does everything short of begging prospective investors to hold off until a better starting point arises. When this occurs, allocators should heed the stop sign.

Kingsford Capital Management[4]

Mike Wilkins and Dave Scially founded Kingsford Capital in 2001. The firm specialized in short-selling U.S. equities and particularly in discovering frauds. Conducting extensive research on companies and the litany of nefarious characters that populated what Kingsford dubbed "the SEC catch and release program," the firm developed a reputation as a gifted fraud hunter and an alpha generator in very challenging times to be a short seller.

Mike and Dave recognized from the beginning that the strategy had capacity constraints. With a larger pool of assets, its best small-cap ideas would get diluted, and they could thoroughly research only a finite number of ideas. Kingsford trained two additional portfolio managers and began allocating its capital among the four. By 2005, it nevertheless began to feel the strains of too much capital and soft closed to new investors.

Kingsford tried to slow the pace of its growth, but demand from existing clients in the midst of a bull market continued apace. Mike and Dave found that almost every client wanted Kingsford to stop growing and potentially give back capital, so long as they weren't the recipient of the capital return. Kingsford had difficulty reconciling this negative externality. Despite struggling to put capital to work most effectively, the fund made money amidst rising equity markets in each of 2005, 2006, and 2007, further bolstering its clients' confidence in the firm.

Throughout a very strong year in 2008, Mike and Dave knew they had to shrink the capital base that had grown to $2 billion in assets. Rather than force feed a return of capital and potentially upset all of their clients, they decided to modestly raise the management fee in the hopes that certain clients would self-select an exit. Starting conversations in the third quarter, Kingsford's returns and assets soared as the capital markets melted down soon thereafter. Through a combination of client liquidity needs and a few clients who got the message, Kingsford returned $800 million during the fourth quarter.

Mike and Dave first asked clients to withdraw capital, then begged and pleaded, and finally tried to force their hands. Kingsford's timing (unfortunately for those remaining) was impeccable and 2009 proved to be the worst year for the strategy on both an absolute and relative basis. In the ensuing bull market years, Kingsford's capital base gradually eroded as clients grew fatigued of the capital protection strategy that lost money steadily in the bull market that commenced in 2009. Despite outperforming its benchmark in every year since inception except for 2009 and maintaining a stellar reputation in its field, by the end of 2014 Kingsford's capital base had shrunk $250 million.

Lonestar Capital[5]

From humble beginnings as a bootstrapped hedge fund in the summer of 1995, Jerome Simon's Lonestar Capital produced extraordinary returns year-in and year-out in its value-oriented strategy that focused on special situations, distressed investing, and the exploitation of leveraged capital structures. With a lean team and modest capital base, Lonestar had a knack for spotting opportunities off the radar screen of larger funds. Lonestar posted at least mid-teens returns every year with low downside volatility.

And then one day, Lonestar gave all the money back.

In the fall of 2006, Jerome announced that he would return all outside capital. Driven in large part by his befuddlement at the lack of resolution in the excesses he saw in capital markets, Jerome believed it was time for him to take a break from investing. He sat on the sidelines during the financial crisis and avoided incurring the pain others experienced.

And in November 2008, Lonestar got back in business.

Jerome recognized that a sizable and compelling opportunity existed in distressed investing following the financial crisis. He picked up right where he left off, rehiring his top two deputies and filling out the rest of the organization. Lonestar printed money in 2009, but thereafter found itself discombobulated in an environment driven by government policymakers. After a few fits and starts in the ensuing years, Lonestar returned investor capital for the second time at the end of 2014.

Looking backward, it is easy to claim that certain managers gave adequate warnings about troubled times ahead in the markets. The more interesting question involves what action to take in real time. Jerome recently returned investor capital a second time—in part due to reasons specific to his firm and in part due to challenges in generating satisfactory returns that he suspects will not go away soon. He is not alone in throwing in the towel of late. In recent years, Chris Shumway closed Shumway Capital, Ian McKinnon retired from Ziff Brothers Investments, John Kleinheintz closed Kleinheintz Capital, Stanley Drukenmiller converted Duquesne Capital to a family office, Jeff Vinik closed Vinik Asset Management, and a host of other long-standing, successful managers closed up shop to manage their own money. Perhaps one day allocators will look back at these actions as a warning call to take action.

Lesson for Managers

Share Your Honest Assessment of the Opportunity Set in Good Times and Bad

Managers are familiar with the paradox that capital is most scarce when investment opportunities are most plentiful. One way to prepare to access capital at critical junctures is to build credibility by sharing your outlook even when opportunities are less robust.

Increasingly, allocators are decomposing their hedge fund portfolios in an effort to access best ideas less expensively. The next time around managers might be pleasantly surprised to find the appetite among allocators increasing when the chips are down.

Lesson for Allocators

When You Fall in Love, Take Your Time

Allocators need not act with expediency when a manager is closing. Surges in demand often follow unusually strong periods of performance. A better starting date may arise to invest in the same manager once performance cools off. Allocators should be patient when building a portfolio of small managers and maintain relationships with their favorite funds, even if those managers are closed for the time being.

CROSSING THE VELVET ROPE

"Good things come to those who wait."

—Proverb

An allocator loves when a manager closes his fund, so long as the allocator has already established a full position in the manager. Allocators not yet invested in the manager may find that patience is warranted and rewarded even in the face of an apparent "now or never" decision.

Very few funds remain permanently closed. A well-placed inquiry might allow an allocator to enter a previously closed fund at a propitious time. Even venerable, long-closed funds have demonstrated an appetite for new capital when the opportunity set appears most attractive. Allocators can be served well by waiting for a manager to wave a green flag.

Like entering a prestigious nightclub in New York City, the velvet rope gets lifted at a time when the appetite to enter has faded. An allocator should prepare well in advance to take advantage of such opportunities.

Brand-Name Openings: Baupost Group, Greenlight Capital, and Elliot Management

The once-in-a-blue-moon opportunity for certain investors to invest in Seth Klarman's Baupost Group occurred in the midst of the malaise in 2008. Seth launched Baupost in 1982 and for two decades managed money for only a handful of his original clients, predominantly a select group of high-net-worth individuals. In the late 1990s, Seth handpicked a small number of highly regarded endowments to join the partnership and enable Baupost to compete on a larger scale.

After eight years with its doors closed, the onset of the financial crisis unearthed a wealth of value investment opportunities that Seth and his team hadn't seen in decades. Baupost opened its doors for existing clients and select endowments and foundations in the spring of 2008 and raised $4 billion.[6]

Baupost is one of the most extreme examples of a "hard-closed" fund, having remained that way for almost its entire 30-year history. Yet at a key moment in time, it became available for certain allocators who were positioned to move quickly.

More recently, another venerable and oft-closed hedge fund, Greenlight Capital, decided to open its doors when a less earth-shattering quake hit equities in October 2014. In its correspondence to investors, chief investment officer David Einhorn cited a breadth of opportunities created by the volatility of markets as the cause for welcoming new capital for the first time in two years.[7]

Paul Singer's Elliot Management took a different approach to prepare for tough times. Rather than wait for the market to yield opportunities, on a number of occasions Elliot raised money through commitments for future investments.[8] Elliot aligned its interest with both its direct client relationships and their governance boards, getting the entire decision-making body prepared for an unknowable date in the future. Should particularly difficult times arise, as Paul contends they will,[9] Elliot knows it will have capital available to invest. It wisely bucked the deer-in-the-headlights tendency that some allocators face in a moment of market panic.

Baupost, Greenlight, and Elliot, while far from small, shine a light on how to make allocations in the proper flow. Rather than chasing recent returns, these managers engendered sufficient confidence among allocators to call for additional funds after a period of weaker returns when future opportunities appeared bright.

Lesson for Allocators

When Managers Call for the Ball, Listen; When They Run for the Hills, Proceed with Caution

Allocators are often most effective when they move slowly and let their manager selections play out over time. By paying careful attention day in and day out, allocators can get attuned to major turning points in markets. Sometimes these shifts prove to be actionable investment opportunities, like when tightly closed funds open. Other times, they should be a call to batten down the hatches, like when a manager puts up a stop sign.

MAKING DECISIONS

"I know it when I see it."

—Justice Potter Stewart, Supreme Court

Each time I have had the opportunity to speak at an industry conference, an audience member inevitably asks the question of how I go about picking managers. The process of manager selection blends science and art, and draws upon experience, judgment, and pattern recognition. Many talented, hardworking young managers populate the investment world, almost all of whom do not fulfill their asset raising ambitions. Rather than articulate in detail the commoditized components of science that characterize my filters, I answer queries by saying that picking managers is akin to former Supreme Court Justice Stewart's assessment of pornography—you know it when you see it.

The patterns that repeat in successful small funds are often quite different from those in larger ones. Initially, managers carry the weight of asset growth over their head. Marketing and client service becomes an integral and continuous allocation of time. Big funds have long since figured out how to manage their time efficiently and effectively; smaller ones may struggle with this balance. Allocators to small funds cannot shy away from this reality without foregoing the opportunity to earn the higher returns many academic studies have shown that young funds generate. Allocators to small funds need to appreciate the challenges these managers face in raising capital and use those lessons to assess how a particular manager is handling the necessary evils of growing his firm.

Building and managing a team is an underappreciated driver of investment success. An allocator needs to see through what a fund is today to what he believes it will be in the future, because most small funds do not have sufficient resources to recruit and retain the talent they want. Along the way, allocators can monitor the patterns that generally lead organizations to thrive. Managers with a single decision maker, proper delegation to team members, willingness to make staffing changes, and a measured pace of growth make it through a screening filter.

Formulating an investment strategy and implementing the strategy are not static processes. Managers start out with a sensible plan in mind, and later encounter tensions and contradictions when forks in the road force them to deviate from the plan. In the words of boxer Mike Tyson, "everyone has a plan 'til they get punched in the mouth." Designing a strategy that fully resonates with the manager, getting capital put to work in the early going, and balancing opportunism are small subsets of the challenges a manager will face. Each allocator needs to get a clear picture in his mind of "his type of fund" and how that fund will thread the needle through the growth trajectory it will face.

Allocators regularly emphasize the importance of process over performance, but ultimately investing is a performance game. When it comes to the bottom line, many allocators dramatically underappreciate the role of luck. Going beyond top line performance to skill assessment can lead an allocator to hunt for managers well positioned to perform in the future, which may not be the same ones that performed well in the past.

Finally, despite a larger and savvier community of allocators, each one must overcome behavioral biases. We all have the tendency to chase returns, and yet we find ways to justify those decisions with a healthy rationale—about the unique talent, the need to get in before the fund closes, or the continuing attractive underlying investment opportunity. On the other side of the spectrum, allocators tend to exit underperforming funds, with sensible reasons in tow. A manager may have other outflows that could impact future returns, it may have encountered previously articulated risks in the strategy, or it may have experienced team turnover.

All of these rationales may be correct and deterministic of future underperformance, but they also happen to get raised at the very moment in time when a fund is struggling. The funny thing about behavioral faults is that they occur despite our knowledge of their existence. It all is quite fascinating, and collectively, we still can't get out of the way. In all my years doing this, I've only rarely encountered situations when allocators exit an outperforming fund or enter an underperforming one.

Lesson for Managers

When You Strip Away the Label, an Allocator's Job Is a Lot Like Yours

Security selection and manager selection are composed of entirely different sets of sourcing and analysis, but the similarities in the two investment styles far outweigh their differences. Appreciating the blend of art and science, pattern recognition, process, performance pressures, and behavioral biases faced by allocators can improve a manager's understanding of the apparent black box at work by those sitting across the table in a presentation. By gaining an understanding of the allocator perspective, managers are better situated to meet their needs.

Lesson for Allocators

Learn from the Best by Applying Your Managers' Best Practices to Your Investment Process

Each allocator develops his own process and set of criteria to evaluate funds. While no two are alike, every allocator can improve his process by drawing on the best practices of the managers he most admires. We are all investors working together toward a common goal of generating uncommon risk-adjusted returns.

8

PARTING THOUGHTS

Investors acquire experience from the repeated practice of their trade. The lessons in this work emanated from my observations of hundreds of hedge funds over a decade and half. Many of the same lessons also impacted the manager allocation business I helped create. Whether raising capital, designing an investment strategy, delivering performance, or working with a team, the parallels between hedge fund investing and allocation are far greater than their differences.

Lots of enterprising 30-somethings aspire to build their own investment organizations. The lessons from history teach that the ones most likely to succeed are those with a strong pedigree, a track record of success, and, most importantly, a deep passion for both the markets and for competing at a high level. The law of large numbers dictates that only a few of the many talented people who set out launch new funds will succeed, but putting the right steps in place can increase a manager's probability of success.

The first step in the process is attracting capital. A manager's path of success—from his education and extracurricular activities through each stage of his professional career—establishes a track record and indicator of potential success. A manager actively engaged in the startup process should think carefully about the signals he sends to prospects. The manner of approach, his poise in an initial meeting, his ability to listen, and his preparedness to follow-through in the marketing process are all factors in raising money.

Once off the ground, managers may find a pattern in the way allocators behave. Early adopters provide capital

for a fund launch. Before long and with some initial investment success, a manager may discover that allocators flock
together like birds of a feather. Managers can find ways
to leverage the buzz among these flocking birds to build
momentum in their fund-raising.

Another key step in the process is creating a thriving
organization. Many start-up managers have not previously had entrepreneurial experience and fail to appreciate the challenges that await. A manager must attract
great people, build an operational infrastructure, conduct
research on securities, and raise capital all at the same
time. A successful manager often figures out important
lessons, such as dedicating a single person to serve as
portfolio manager, balancing authority and delegation,
rectifying suboptimal personnel decisions, and growing
at a measured pace. All along, a manager needs to spend
time learning about himself, his people, and the organization growing before his eyes.

The production of investment returns arises from a mix
of ingredients including the team, strategy, and process.
When the parts blend effectively, performance may follow.
A manager should choose the investment strategy most
suited to his passion, recognizing the challenges regardless
of the strategy he selects. Allocators ultimately need to see

results, and a manager focusing intently on process stands the best chance to produce satisfactory outcomes.

Most of the lessons in this work focus on the first few years of a start-up hedge fund. Should a manager successfully navigate the launch period, he will find variations of the same issues in different stages of his firm's life. When the start-up phase settles down, a manager will turn his attention to growth (new marketing channels, new products, improved processes), the team (retaining high performers, upgrading low performers, motivation and alignment, and culture), investment strategy (ebb and flow of markets and returns, communication to clients), and of course, performance. Each new stage of development brings in a host of new challenges, and hedge funds rarely get a chance to take a deep breath and stand still.

• • •

Sitting in between clients and managers has afforded me a front-row seat to the development and institutionalization of the hedge fund industry. The more time I have spent in my chair, the more I saw how similar my role was to that of hedge fund managers. They faced the same challenges of building a business and generating performance that I did, with a comparable set of risks in the evolution of our respective subindustries.

I encourage you to reflect on your investing journey and the many connections it has to others that have come before you and will come after. Together, we are creating the lessons of history.

AUTHOR'S DISCLAIMER

• • •

Nonsolicitation. This publication is an informational document and does not constitute an offer to sell or a solicitation to purchase any securities in any entity organized, controlled, affiliated, or managed by Ted Seides, Protégé Partners or their affiliates, or any other manager discussed herein, and therefore may not be relied upon in connection with any offer or sale of securities.

In addition, this book is a narrative, and information about the events, persons, relationships, or occurrences may be incomplete; this book does not contain any material terms pertinent to an investment decision, including important disclosures of conflicts and risk factors associated with an investment in any fund. This book in and of itself should not form the basis for any investment decision.

No Liability. No responsibility or liability is assumed by the author for any injury, damage, or financial loss sustained to persons or property from the use of this information, personal or otherwise, either directly or indirectly. All liability from any use or misuse of the operation of any methods, strategies, instructions, or ideas contained herein is the sole responsibility of the reader. The author shall not be liable for any loss of profit or any other commercial damages, including but not limited to special, incidental, consequential, or other damages, under any theory.

All trademarks and brands referred to in this book are for illustrative purposes only, are the property of their respective owners, and are not affiliated with this publication in any way.

Disclaimer of Warranty. Ted Seides makes no representations or warranties with respect to the accuracy or completeness of the contents of this book and specifically disclaim any implied warranties of merchantability or fitness for a particular purpose. The advice and strategies contained herein may not be suitable for your situation.

No Fiduciary Relationship. Ted Seides is not acting and does not purport to act in any way as an adviser or in a fiduciary capacity vis-à-vis any investor in any fund mentioned in this book.

This publication is designed to provide accurate and authoritative information in regard to the subject matter covered. It is sold with the understanding that Ted Seides is not engaged in rendering legal or accounting advice, or other professional services. It is strongly suggested that any reader of this book obtain independent advice in relation to any investment, financial, legal, tax, accounting, or regulatory issues discussed in this book.

Risk Disclosure. Analyses and opinions contained in this book may be based on assumptions that, if altered, can change the analyses or opinions expressed. Nothing contained in this book shall constitute any representation or warranty as to future performance of any financial instrument, credit, currency rate, or other market or economic measure.

Financial instruments and investment opportunities discussed or referenced in this book may not be suitable for all investors, and potential investors must make an independent assessment of the appropriateness of any transaction in light of their own objectives and circumstances, including the possible risk and benefits of entering into such a transaction.

Sole Authorship. The views and opinions expressed in this book are those of Ted Seides and do not reflect the view, policy, or position of Protégé Partners, its affiliates, or any other fund or manager described herein. Examples of stories in this book are only examples and should not be utilized in real-world analytic products, as they are based only on very limited and dated open-source information.

ABOUT THE
AUTHOR

Ted Seides is the son of a teacher and a psychiatrist. Perhaps by genetic disposition, he became passionate about sharing his insights and investing in people. Whether working with money managers, coaching his kids' sports teams, or helping with nonprofits, Ted takes gratification from these pursuits.

From 2002 until 2015, Ted was a founder of Protégé Partners, LLC and served as president and co-chief investment officer. Protégé is an alternative investment firm that invests in small and specialized hedge funds on an arm's-length and seed basis. Ted built the firm's investment process and managed the sourcing, research, and due diligence of its portfolios. Ted worked actively with each of Protégé's 40 seed managers. In 2010, Larry Kochard and Cathleen Ritterheiser profiled Ted in the book *Top Hedge Fund Investors: Stories, Strategies, and Advice* (Wiley, 2010).

Ted began his career in 1992, spending five years under the tutelage of David Swensen at the Yale University Investments Office. He focused on external public equity managers and internal fixed-income portfolio management. Following business school, Ted spent two years investing directly at a hedge fund and private equity firm.

With aspirations to demonstrate the salutary benefits of hedge funds on institutional portfolios to a broad audience, Ted made a nonprofitable wager with Warren Buffett that pitted the 10-year performance of the S&P 500 against a selection of five hedge fund of funds from 2008 to 2017.

Ted writes a blog for the CFA Institute's Enterprising Investor (www.blogs.cfainstitute.org/investor) and has authored pieces for *Institutional Investor,* Harvard Business School Publishing, and the late Peter L. Bernstein's *Economics and Portfolio Strategy.*

Ted is a periodic commentator on Deirdre Bolton's *Risk and Reward* on Fox Business News, has appeared with

David Brancaccio on American Public Media's *Marketplace Morning Report*, and speaks at client and industry conferences on the topics of talent identification, skill assessment, investment process, portfolio construction, and the bet with Warren Buffett.

Ted sits on the board of trustees of the Greenwich Roundtable° and is a trustee and member of the investment committee of the Wenner-Gren Foundation. He is a member of the Founder's Circle of Cycle for Survival and the board of Technocademy, and previously was a board member of Citizen Schools–New York. Ted holds a BA in economics and political science, cum laude with distinction in the major, from Yale University, and an MBA with honors from Harvard Business School.

NOTES

Introduction

1. "Global Billion Dollar Club." *Hedge Fund Intelligence*, September 22, 2014.

2. Stefanova, Katina, "The Looming Talent Crisis: Are Hedge Funds Due for a Wake-Up Call?" www.forbes.com, April 25, 2015.

3. J. P. Morgan Capital Introduction Group, "Institutional Investor Survey—2015."

4. Ellis, Charles D., "The Rise and Fall of Performance Investing." *Financial Analysts Journal,* July/August 2014.

5. Bernstein, Peter L., "What Happens if We're Wrong?" *New York Times,* June 22, 2008.

6. Train, John, *The Money Masters*. New York, NY: HarperBusiness, 1994.

Chapter 2

1. For example, Bank of America Merrill Lynch Prime Brokerage Consulting, "Guide to Starting a Hedge Fund," Q3 2015.

Chapter 3

1. McCarthy, Jerome E., *Basic Marketing: A Managerial Approach*. Homewood, IL: Irwin, 1964.

2. Lauterborn, Bob, "New Marketing Litany: Four Ps Passe: C-Words Take Over." *Advertising Age*, October 1, 1990.

3. Schwed, Fred Jr., *Where Are the Customers' Yachts?* New York, NY: John Wiley & Sons, 1995. Copyright 1940.

4. Buffett, Warren E., "The Superinvestors of Graham-and-Doddsville." *Hermes: Columbia Business School Magazine*, May 1984.

5. Loomis, Carol L., "Buffett's Big Bet," *Fortune*, June 23, 2008.

6. Dooley, Roger, "First Impressions: Incredibly Quick to Form, Slow to Change." www.forbes.com/sites/rogerdooley/2014/05/19/first-impressions.

7. Rajesh Sachdeva, interview with the author, March 6, 2015.

8. Interview with the author, January 19, 2015. Pocock Capital and Joe Rantz are fictional names taken from Daniel James Brown's *Boys in the Boat*, New York: Penguin Books, 2013. Some of the information, including the principal's background and investment strategy, has been changed.

9. Jeremy Green, interview with the author, March 12, 2015.

10. Craig Nerenberg and Josh Kaufman, interview with the author, December 11, 2014.

11. Befitting the firm, the only mention of Brenner West Capital in the mainstream press occurred in a *Wall Street Journal* article on September 7, 2011, entitled "Some Hedge Funds, to Stay Nimble, Reject New Investors."

12. At the Boys & Girls Harbor Investment Conference in 2011, Bill Ackman introduced Craig by stating that his father, children, and he were all Brenner West Capital limited partners.

13. Fournier, Susan, and Robert Dolan, "Launching the BMW Z3 Roadster." Harvard Business School Case 9-597-002, 1997.

14. Rantala, Ville, "How Do Investment Ideas Spread through Social Interation? Evidence from a Ponzi Scheme." Aalto University School of Business, March 16, 2015. www.ssrn.com/abstract=2579847.

15. Keynes, John Maynard, *The General Theory of Employment, Interest and Money*. London, England: Palgrave Macmillan, 1936.

16. Steinbrugge, Don, "Hedge Fund Branding Continues to Drive a Majority of Asset Flows." August 12, 2014. www.agecroftpartners.com.

17. Steinbrugge, Don, "Momentum in Asset Growth Is Vital to Successfully Raising Hedge Fund Assets." 2013. www.agecroftpartners.com.

18. Andrew Goldman, interview with the author, April 10, 2015.

19. Philip Timon, interview with the author, November 13, 2014.

Chapter 4

1. Jason Karp, panel at Milken Institute Global Conference, "The Intangibles of Building a Great Hedge Fund: People as an Asset Class," April 27, 2015.

2. Carol Morley and Dana Galin, interview with the author, May 13, 2015.

3. Katina Stefanova, interview with Carol Morley, "The Looming Talent Crisis: Are Hedge Funds Due for a Wake-Up Call?" www.forbes.com, April 25, 2015.

4. Pink, Daniel H., *Drive: The Surprising Truth About What Motivates Us.* New York, NY: Riverhead Books, 2011.

5. "Huge Hedge Fund Launched Successfully Under Eric Mindich," *Wall Street Journal*, November 3, 2004. www.wsj.com.

6. "Eton Park's Hendel Is Returning to Morgan Stanley," *Wall Street Journal*, October 4, 2006. www.wsj.com.

7. Erez Kalir and Craig Perry, interviews with the author, April 16 and 17, 2015.

8. Davide Serra, interview with the author, March 3, 2015.

9. Steve Galbraith, interview with the author, March 13, 2015.

10. Interview with the author, March 30, 2015. Farthings Capital and Sebastian Clifton are fictional names taken from Jeffrey Archer's *The Clifton Chronicles*. New York: St. Martin's Press, 2015. Some of the information, including AUM, performance, strategy, and dates, has been changed.

11. DiChristoper, Tom, "Tony Robbins: The One Thing All Top Investors Do." www.cnbc.com, November 14, 2014.

Chapter 5

1. Cohen, Randy, Christopher Polk, and Bernhard Silli, "Best Ideas." SSRN ID 136427, March 15, 2010.

2. Peter Carlin, interview with the author, April 6, 2015.

3. Dalbar, "Dalbar's 2014 Quantitative Analysis of Investor Behavior." www.dalbar.com.

4. Bartley, Aaron, and Kevin Connor, "How Robert Rubin's Bright-Eyed Protégés Came to Dominate Wall Street." www.alternet.org. March 15, 2009.

5. Rittereiser, Cathleen, and Lawrence Kochard, "A Legendary Wildcat Strike." *Top Hedge Fund Investors*. Hoboken, NJ: John Wiley & Sons, 2010, p 56.

6. Aley, James, "Wall Street's King Quant David Shaw's Secret Formulas Pile Up Money, Now He Wants a Piece of the Net." *Fortune*, February 5, 1996.

7. Andy Redleaf, interview with the author, March 12, 2015.

8. Lewis, Michael, *The Big Short*. New York, NY: W. W. Norton & Company, 2011.

9. Barclays Prime Services Hedge Fund Pulse, "The Curious Case of Converts." November 2013.

10. "Pine River Kicks Off Global Convertible Arbitrage Funds." www.institutionalinvestorsalpha.com. June 3, 2002.

11. "Shifting into High Gear." www.institutionalinvestorsalpha.com. March 15, 2004.

12. Lewis, *The Big Short;* and Zuckerman, Gregory, *The Greatest Trade Ever.* New York, NY: Crown Business, 2010.

13. Lewis, "In the Land of the Blind," "The Long Quiet," and "Two Men in a Boat." *The Big Short.*

14. Interviews with the author, March 23 and 27, 2015. Edgemeont Capital, Ken Guch, and Dan Mully are fictional names taken from my high school and four close friends who were classmates.

15. Swensen, David F. *Pioneering Portfolio Management*, New York, NY: Free Press, 2000, p. 114.

16. Jason Karp, interview with the author, January 6, 2015.

17. Gawande, Atul. *The Checklist Manifesto: How to Get Things Right.* New York, NY: Metropolitan Books, 2009.

Chapter 6

1. Montier, James, "The World's Dumbest Idea." www.gmo.com, December 1, 2014, discusses the negative impact of a focus on shareholder value on corporate America. His data describing the absence of corporate investment and short tenures of CEOs is driven by a short-term performance mind-set.

2. Steve Diamond, interview with the author, March 2, 2015.

3. Steve worked for Antoine van Agtmael, the founder of Emerging Markets Investors, who coined the phrase "emerging market" during his time at the World Bank in the 1980s and Hari Hariharan at New World, who was considered among the brightest minds in emerging-markets investing.

4. Steve Diamond, interview with the author, July 1, 2003.

5. Interview with the author, April 8, 2015. Derek Abruzzese and Stoneham Capital are fictional names taken from a close friend from college and his hometown.

6. Interview with the author, April 6, 2015. Dubuque Capital and Ray Kinsella, Terence Mann, and Archie Griffin are fictional names taken from the movie *Field of Dreams*, Universal Pictures, 1989. Some of the information, including the details of the private investment, has been changed.

7. www.hf-implode.com/imploded/fund_AskinCapital Management_1994.

8. Abelson, Reed, "Pssst ... We Have No Problems at This Hedge Fund. Really." *New York Times*, October 18, 1998.

9. Alex Klabin, interview with the author, April 11, 2015.

10. Attributed to the Roman philosopher Seneca.

11. Siddharth Thacker, interview with the author, March 31, 2015.

Chapter 7

1. Ruiz, Don Miguel, *The Four Agreements*. San Rafael, CA; Amber-Allen Publishing, 1997, p. 48.

2. Gerald Kerner's white paper, "Hedge Funds: Problems Under the Hood" (January 2014) lays out many of the problems in partnership agreements.

3. Buffett, Warren E., "Letter to Shareholders of Berkshire Hathaway," 1997.

4. Mike Wilkins, interview with the author, March 22, 2015.

5. Jerome Simon, interview with the author, April 3, 2015.

6. Stein, Charles, "Klarman Tops Griffin as Investors Hunt for 'Margin of Safety.'" *BloombergBusiness*, June 11, 2010.

7. Foxman, Simone, "Einhorn's Greenlight to Reopen Hedge Fund to New Capital." *Bloomberg*, October 16, 2014.

8. Hussain, Tabinda. "Paul Singer's Elliot Raises $3.3 Billion in New Capital." www.valuewalk.com. October 8, 2013.

9. Copeland, Rob. "Bears Who Won Big During Finance Crisis Are Growling Again." *Wall Street Journal*, July 31, 2014.

INDEX

A

Abruzzese, Derek, 135–136

Agecroft Partners, 51–53

Algebris Investments, 80–81

Allocator relationships, 153–181
  decision making, 177–181
    lesson for allocators, 181
    lesson for managers, 180–181
  exiting, 167–173
    Kingsford Capital Management,
      168–170
    lesson for allocators, 173
    lesson for managers, 172–173
    Lonestar Capital, 170–172
  influencing outcomes, 154–157
    lesson for allocators, 157
    lesson for managers, 157
  opportunities to invest, taking
      advantage of, 173–177
    brand-name openings, 174–176
    lesson for allocators, 176–177
  preparing for challenges, 164–167
    lesson for allocators, 167
    lesson for managers, 166–167

  terms, 158–164
    expenses, 159
    fees, 158–159
    lesson for allocators, 164
    lesson for managers, 163–164
    liquidity, 160–163
    transparency, 160

Allocators, lessons for
  allocator relationships, 5–6, 157,
      164, 167, 173, 176–177, 181
  decision making, 181
  influencing outcomes, 157
  mental model, adjusting, 167
  opportunities to invest, taking
      advantage of, 176–177
  patience, 173
  terms, 164

attracting capital, 4, 29, 42, 48, 54,
      58–59, 63–64
  assessing outlook, 63–64
  investing in early stages of
      fund, 42
  thinking like a manager, 48
  time management, 29

Allocators (*continued*)
    timing of investment, 54,
      58–59
    investment performance, 5,
      133–134, 137, 143–144
    focusing on what is important,
      143–144
    interactions with manager,
      133–134
    luck, role of, 149–150
    performance chasing, 137
    investment strategy, 5, 100, 117,
      122–123, 128
    communicating with managers,
      117, 122–123
    goals and assessment of
      performance, 100
    paying attention to process,
      128
    team, 4, 73, 76, 82, 90–91, 93–95
    bringing new teams together,
      76
    dual portfolio manager
      structures, 82
    personnel changes, 90–91
    prioritizing talent development,
      73
    scrutinizing assumptions,
      94–95
AQR Capital, 47
Axonic Capital, 146

B
Baupost Group, 174–176
Bernstein, Peter, xx
BMW Z3 Roadster, launch of, 59
Bootstrapping, 30–34
    Flowering Tree Investment
      Management, 31–34
Brenner West Capital, 44–47

Bridgewater Associates, 47
Buffett, Warren, xiv, 165
    bet with, 15–18
Burry, Michael, 114–116

C
Capital, attracting, 11–64, 184
    classic chicken-and-egg problem,
      29–42
    bootstrapping, 30–34
    discounted terms/founders'
      shares, 38–41
    lesson for allocators, 42
    lesson for managers, 41–42
    seed capital, 34–37
    diversification, 59–64
    Endowment Capital Group,
      61–62
    lesson for allocators, 63–64
    lesson for managers, 63
    leveraging the buzz, 49–54
    Agecroft Partners, 51–53
    lesson for allocators, 54
    lesson for managers, 53
    momentum, building on, 54–59
    Seven Locks Capital, 56–58
    lesson for allocators, 58–59
    lesson for managers, 58
    raising capital, 43–47
    Brenner West Capital, 44–47
    lesson for allocators, 48
    lesson for managers, 47
    signals of success, 12–29
    approaching prospects, 14–15
    bet with Warren Buffett, 15–18
    lessons for managers, 25
    signals in marketing, 25–27
    signals in operations, 27–28
    Circular File, 18–22
Carlin, Peter, 103–104

Carr, Charlie, 103–104
Clifton, Sebastian, 87–89
Convertible arbitrage, survivors in, 112–114

D
Diamond, Steve, 131–132
Direct lending in 2007–2008, 142–143
Discounted terms/founders' shares, 38–41
Diversification, 59–64
Drukenmiller, Stanley, 172
Dubuque Captial, 140–141
Durst, Greg, 67

E
Edgemont Partners, 118–121
Einhorn, David, 175
Ellington Capital, 146
Elliot Management, 174–176
Ellis, Charley, xx
Endowment Capital Group, 61–62
Estekene Capital, 103–104

F
Farthings Capital, 87–89
Flowering Tree Investment Management, 31–34
Founder's shares, 38–41

G
Galbraith, Steve, 84–85
Galin, Dana, 67
Garg, Neeraj, 67
Gating, 161–163
Goldman, Andrew, 56–57
Graham, Archie, 140–141

Grantham, Jeremy, xiv
Green, Jeremy, 39–41
Greenlight Capital, 174–176
Guch Ken, 118–121

H
Halet, Eric, 80–81
Hedge fund, starting, 7–10
    reasons for, 8–9
Hedge fund industry, structure of, xvii
Herring Creek Capital, 84–86
Housing collapse, winners in, 114

I
Imprint Group, 67–72
    success strategies for building a high-performing team, 69–72
    talent crisis in asset management, 67–68
Investment performance, 129–152
    luck, role of, 144–150
        lesson for allocators, 149–150
        lesson for managers, 149
        postcrisis distressed residential mortgage funds, 145–146
        Senator Investment Group, 147–148
    manager's best performance month, 150–152
        Signpost Capital, 151–152
    performance reports, 130–134
        lesson for allocators, 133–134
        lesson for managers, 133
        Tiedemann Emerging Markets Fund, 131–132
    reaching for return, 138–144
        direct lending in 2007–2008, 142–143
        Dubuque Capital, 140–141

Index

Investment performance (*continued*)
  lesson for allocators, 143
  lesson for managers, 143–144
sustaining performance, 134–137
  lesson for allocators, 137
  lesson for managers, 136–137
  Stoneham Captial, 135–136
Investment strategy, 97–128
  flexibility and style drift, 106–117
    convertible arbitrage, survivors
      in, 112–114
    housing collapse, winners in,
      114
    lesson for managers, 116
    multistrategy hedge funds,
      108–109
    Scion Capital, 114–116
    Whitebox Advisors, 110–112
  focused strategy, 117–123
    Edgemont Partners, 118–121
    lesson for allocators, 122–123
    lesson for managers, 122
  following instincts, 98–100
    lesson for allocators, 100
    lesson for managers, 99
  investment process, building
    blocks of, 123–128
    lesson for allocators, 128
    lesson for managers, 127–128
    Tourbillon Capital, 125–127
  performing well in early stage,
    100–106
    Estekene Capital, 103–104
    lesson for allocators, 105–106
    lesson for managers, 105

K
Kalir, Erez, 77–79
Karp, Jason, 125–127
Kaufman, Joshua, 44–45

Keynes, John Maynard, 50
Kingsford Capital Management,
    168–170
Kinsella, Ray, 140–141
Klabin, Alex, 147–148
Klarman, Seth, 174–175
Kleinheintz, John, 172

L
Lessons. *See* Allocators, lessons for;
    Managers, lessons for
LibreMax Capital, 146
Lonestar Capital, 170–172
Long-Term Capital Management,
    146, 161

M
Managers, lessons for
  allocator relationships, 3, 157,
    163–164, 166–167,
    172–173, 180–181
    assessment, sharing,
      172–173
    decision making, 180–181
    educating investors, 166–167
    influencing outcomes, 157
    terms, 163–164
  attracting capital, 1–2, 25, 28–29,
    41–42, 47, 53, 58, 63
    approaching prospects, 25
    being prepared in advance, 58
    creating a brand and leveraging
      the buzz, 53
    dedicating resources to
      marketing process, 47
    diversification, 63
    incentives, offering, 41–42
    reflecting/presenting oneself to
      prospective investors,
      28–29

investment performance, 3, 133,
    136–137, 143, 149
  luck, role of, 149
  private investments, avoiding,
    143
  short-term focus, 133
  sustaining performance,
    136–137
investment strategy, 2–3, 99, 116,
    122, 127–128
  communicating frequently with
    clients, 116
  focused strategy, 122
  following instincts, 99
  paying attention to process,
    127–128
team, 2, 72–75, 75–76, 82, 86,
    90–91, 93–95
  challenges of building, 75–76
  drivers of success, staying
    connected to, 93–94
  dual portfolio manager
    structures, 82
  investing in people, 72–75
  making necessary changes, 90
  "nice guys" as managers, 86
Mann, Terence, 140–141
McKinnon, Ian, 172
Mindich, Eric, 74–75
Morley, Carol, 67
Mully, Dan, 118–121
Multistrategy hedge funds,
    108–109

N
Nerenberg, Craig, 44–45
Noble, Alasdair, 46

O
One William Street, 146

P
Performance reports, 130–134
Perry, Craig, 77–79
Pocock Capital, 36–38
Postcrisis distressed residential
    mortgage funds, 145–146
Proudlove, Sascha, 67

R
Rantz, Joe, 36–38
Redleaf, Andrew, 110–111
Redmile Group, 39–41
Residential mortgage-backed securities
    (RMBS) funds 145–146
Retirement risk, xviii
Risk management slide, 23–24

S
Sabretooth Capital, 77–79
Sachdeva, Rajesh, 31–34
Scially, Dave, 168
Scion Capital, 114–116
Seed capital, 34–37
  Pocock Capital, 36–38
Seer Capital, 146
Senator Investment Group,
    147–148
Serra, Davide, 80–81
Seven Locks Capital, 56–58
Shumway, Chris, 172
Signpost Capital, 151–152
Silverman, Doug, 147–148
Simon, Jerome, 170–172
Singer, Paul, 175–176
Soros, George, 131
Start-up hedge funds, investing
    in, xv, 153–181. *See also*
    Allocator relationships
Steinbrugge, Don, 51–53, 55–56
Stoneham Capital, 135–136

Story fund investing, 165–166
Swensen, David, xiii, 124

T
Team, 65–96
  building, 66–72
    Imprint Group, 67–73
    lesson for allocators, 73
    lesson for managers, 72
  co–portfolio manager construct,
    76–83
    Algebris Investments, 80–81
    lesson for allocators, 82–83
    lesson for managers, 82
    Sabretooth Capital, 77–79
  "nice guys" as managers, 83–86
    Herring Creek Capital, 84–86
    lesson for managers, 86
  pacing growth, 91–95
    lesson for allocators, 94–95
    lesson for managers, 93–94
  reaching potential, 73–76
    Eton Park Capital, 74–76
    lesson for allocators, 76
    lesson for managers, 75–76

  turnover, 86–91
    Farthings Capital, 87–89
    lesson for allocators, 90–91
    lesson for managers, 90
Terms, 158–164
  expenses, 159
  fees, 158–159
  lesson for allocators, 164
  lesson for managers, 163–164
  liquidity, 160–163
  transparency, 160
Thacker, Siddharth, 151–152
Tiedemann Emerging Markets
    Fund, 131–132
Tilden Park Capital, 146
Timon, Philip, 61–62

V
Vinik, Jeff, 172

W
Whitebox Advisors, 110–112
Wilkins, Mike, 168–170
Yale University, xiii–xiv